If any one desire to be first,
the same shall be last of all,
and SERVANT OF ALL.

Paperback cover art design: Mosaic from the Cappella della "Casa incontri cristiani" a Capiago, Unction of Bethany 2006.

Mark's Gospel: A Devotional Commentary

The print book uses Ryman Eco font which utilises 33% less ink than most prints to support eco friendly fonts toward responsible stewardship of earth's resources entrusted to us by the living God of Abraham, Isaac and Jacob who made this world for flourishing.

Servant of All

Anyone who has left everything for My sake,
and the gospel's shall receive an hundredfold now in this time,
houses, brothers, sisters, mothers, children, and lands,
WITH PERSECUTIONS;
and in the world to come eternal life.
But many that are first
shall be last;
and the last first.

Son of Man

At least it hides the face partly well, so you have the apparent face, the apple, hiding the visible but hidden, the face of the person. It's something that happens constantly. EVERYTHING WE SEE HIDES ANOTHER THING, WE ALWAYS WANT TO SEE WHAT IS HIDDEN BY WHAT WE SEE. There is an interest in that which is hidden and which the visible does not show us. This interest can take the form of a quite intense feeling, a sort of conflict, one might say, between the visible that is hidden and the visible that is present. (Rene Magritte)

Son of Man

One who aspires to greatness
shall be a servant,
ONE WHO DESIRES TO BE FIRST
SHALL BE SLAVE OF ALL.
For the Son of Man came
not to be served, but to serve,
and to give His life
a ransom for many.

Mark 10:44-45

God shall raise up a Prophet from among the Israelites
like Moses and they shall hear all things He says.

Foreword

This devotional commentary serves as an introductory guide on Christianity's beginnings and how John Mark portrays the ministry of Jesus of Nazareth as the Son of Man, fulfilling a 700 year prophecy of Israel's coming Messiah, Son of David, amidst Jewish expectations of deliverance from Roman rule at the dawn of the first century AD. For Moses predicted, more than 700 years before Isaiah, God shall raise up a Prophet from among the Israelites like him, and they shall hear all things He says to them. All the prophets from Samuel foretold the covenant God made with their fathers to Abraham, In your Seed shall all kindreds of the earth be blessed.

As topical study, cross referencing similar subject matter contain in the holy books of Christian faith in the TaNaKh (Torah, Prophets, Writings) & New Testament books collectively known as holy scriptures written over a span of 1,500 years by 40 writers inspired by God's Spirit. Therefore, content are mainly compiled from the synoptic gospels in KJV unless otherwise indicated and contain little personal commentary for each reading is a coherent conversation with biblical writers as scripture interprets scripture.

Followers of Messiah Jesus remember our present time on earth is in transit (in the world but not of the world), rendering to Caesar what belongs to Caesar and to God what belongs to God. We are living in between times looking back to the future with the Holy Spirit reminding, teaching us and guiding our way in the last days.

Finally, it provides a basic structure of discipleship for practitioners in faithful living for good: commending us to God through the word of His grace to bear true witness of the great deliverance of Messiah Jesus in His momentous sacrifice to bring many sons and daughters of God to share the Father's joy and glory, establishing His kingdom life in us to make disciples of all nations.

the crooked shall be made straight,
and the rough places made good.

Old Testament Back Story

For unto us a Child is born, a Son is given: the government shall be on His shoulder: His Name shall be called Wonderful, Counsellor, The mighty God, The everlasting Father, The Prince of Peace. His government shall prevail and there shall be no end of peace, on the throne of David, and His kingdom, to order it, and to establish it with justice and righteousness from henceforth even for ever. The zeal of the LORD of hosts will perform this. (Isaiah 9:6-7)

The prophet Isaiah who lived during the times of four kings of Judah (Uzziah, Jotham, Ahaz and Hezekiah) around 800BC prophesied the coming of Messiah Jesus more than 700 years before John the Baptist appeared in the vicinity of Jordan River preaching a message of repentance and water baptism for cleansing of sins to prepare the way for Jesus' wholistic ministry and gospel mission.

John himself was the voice crying in the wilderness:

Prepare ye the way of the LORD, make straight path in the desert a highway for our God. Every valley shall be exalted, and every mountain and hill shall be made low: and the crooked shall be made straight, and the rough places made plain. (Isaiah 40:3-4)

The way of the LORD is the path of righteousness and peace. Though the world in many ways is like a desert in the wilderness, inhospitable and hostile, the Messiah will make straight every crooked path and heart, tempering every rough places of sin-sick, confused and disordered lives, turning them into plain good places.

The Christian outlier encounters Mark's gospel and how its narrative unfolds to present the fulfilment of TaNaKh prophecies as Jesus embark on restoring wholeness to our body, mind and soul: heal our brokenness, pardon our bondage in sins, open our blind eyes to see light from darkness and release us from our bruised oppression to go in peace to love and serve in His Name.

God delight not only in good work but
desire to make us holy and good as He is.

Good News of Good Life

Euangelion is good news or gospel. As used by New Testament writers, is shorthand for the good news of Messiah Jesus, the Son of God who comes proclaiming the gospel of the kingdom of God, fulfilling Old Testament prophecies in the fullness of time.

John the Baptist preach repentance and water baptism for the forgiveness of sin, bearing good fruit in keeping with repentance. Jesus proclaim deliverance and Spirit baptism for God's kingdom reign in our lives, bearing witness in newness of life. The way in to His kingdom is being born again as God's children, for God delight not only in good work but desire to make us holy and good as He is.

It matters not if you are broken, outcast, or despised. Only that you repent, trust and obey His rule and reign. For the kingdom of God, is not meat and drink; but righteousness, and peace, and joy in the Holy Spirit. It is an eschaton (ultimate) reality embodying the ecclesia (congregation) in Messiah existing as community.

Far easier for the childlike and poor to enter in, as compared to the rich and powerful, whom Jesus says has more difficulty entering than a camel passing through a needle's eye. Many invited could not enter in: serving mammon, having darkened minds, savouring men's things; so the door is flung wide open to the deprived and oppressed, whom the world deem as not good enough; maligned, mistreated, and discarded like defective goods.

Without sin, He was made sin for us. Rejected. Betrayed. Crucified. Buried. Risen, on the third day, to give life to anyone who call upon His Name. Anyone in Messiah is a new creation, old life is passing away. The breaking in of a new life, a new beginning beckons. Euangelion: good news of good life. Jesus says, Take My yoke and learn of Me. For I am meek and lowly in heart. You shall find rest for your soul: for My yoke is gracious and My task is light.

Repent, for the kingdom of God
is near and believe the gospel.

Preface

The gospel of Mark is the shortest and earliest of four gospel accounts in the New Testament. Written around 65 AD (just before the Jerusalem temple was destroyed ending the Jewish War) by John Mark as recounted to him by Peter in terse Greek with some Aramaic phrases. It is fast pace, full of realism and distinct for saying Jesus 'is mad' (beside Himself), a two-stage healing of a blind man, an intimate moment with God as Abba Father (Aramaic) in the Garden of Gethsemane in deep anguished prayer as well as a cry by Jesus in Aramaised Hebrew on the cross. A Palestinian Jew.

Mark's gospel may be roughly divided into 3 thematic purposes: 1) Jesus' commission of His disciples to proclaim the gospel of the Kingdom of God; 2) His confirmation fulfilling TaNaKh prophecies of Israel's promised Messiah attested by mighty works, confession by devils He is Son of God, people's recognising Him as Son of David, God's approval of His beloved Son, His self-identity as Son of Man, power to raise the dead, authority over nature and to forgive sins; 3) the passion narratives of His necessary and imminent rejection by the Jewish religious leaders leading to His betrayal, death, burial, and resurrection on the third day.

The extended discussion with Jesus' disciples on suffering in relation to the passion narrative reveals Mark's thrust in clarifying what following Jesus entail. Its hostile and violent opposition from both Jewish elite, religious and political establishment even as the poor, needy and outcasts of society welcome and receives Jesus gladly, makes clear that bearing witness to Jesus and the kingdom of God is filled with both rejection and suffering alongside rewards of entrance and enjoyment of being part of a new community as outliers and kindred of God's everlasting kingdom.

Repent, for the kingdom of God is near and believe the gospel.

offering humble service and patient suffering
before a hurting, hostile and confused world.

Prologue

A certain mood of anticipation accompanies Jesus' proclaiming the gospel of the kingdom of God is mitigated by an atmosphere of secrecy reflected in His constant charge of those who are restored to wholeness not to publish the news of their recovery except to show themselves to the priests as a testimony of God's goodness and grace. Though not always followed as many proclaim openly in uncontainable gratitude to Jesus, its purpose is to allow Jesus to complete His earthly and public ministry to restore and deliver the world from sins, corruption and darkness culminating at His rejection, betrayal, death, burial and resurrection.

The Kingdom of God is neither political nor of this world, contrary to Jewish expectations which Jesus made clear in His reply to the religious establishment ploy to trap Him that we render to Caesar what's Caesar and to God what's God. The kingdom's reign and rule is in the hearts of Jesus' followers to live a life of righteousness, peace and joy in the Holy Spirit, offering humble service and patient suffering before a hurting, hostile and confused world exemplified by His mission that the Son of Man came not to be served but to serve and give His life a ransom for many.

Parables contain kingdom mysteries, revealing not just its hidden but precious value that Jesus emphasise as belonging to His followers even as He explains them while preempting others from being judge prematurely if they hear and reject its invitation thus condemning themselves unwittingly. Mark lay out two key passages (chapters 4 & 13) on rightly hearing and clearly seeing who Jesus is and the gospel of the kingdom of God for truth seekers and outliers in good places. Jesus' final words to His followers in light of His parousia (coming again) amidst troubles and tribulations is to preach good news of good life in His Name, making disciples.

Gospel of Messiah Jesus, the Son of God (1:1-15)

The beginning of the gospel of Messiah Jesus, the Son of God; as it is written in the prophets, Behold, I send My messenger before Your face, who shall prepare Your way before You. The voice of one crying in the wilderness, Prepare the way of the LORD, make His paths straight. John baptise in the wilderness, and preach the baptism of repentance for the forgiveness of sins. There went out to him all the land of Judaea, and Jerusalem, and were all baptised by him in the Jordan river, confessing their sins. John was clothed with camel's hair, with a leather belt on his waist; and he ate locusts and wild honey. He preached, saying, There comes One mightier than I after me, the straps of whose sandals I am not worthy to stoop and untie. I baptised you with water but He shall baptise you with the Holy Spirit. In those days, Jesus came from Nazareth of Galilee, and was baptised by John in the Jordan. Straightaway coming up out of the water, he saw the heavens opened, and the Spirit like a dove descending upon Him. There came a Voice from heaven, saying, You are My beloved Son, in whom I am well pleased. Immediately the Spirit drives Him into the wilderness. He was there in the wilderness forty days, tempted by Satan; and was with the wild beasts; and angels ministered to Him. Soon after John was put in prison, Jesus came to Galilee, preaching the gospel of the kingdom of God, saying, The time is fulfilled, God's kingdom is near: you repent, and believe the gospel.

Therefore the Lord Himself shall give you a sign; Behold, a virgin shall conceive, and bear a Son, and shall call His Name Immanuel, which means, God is with us. Butter and honey shall He eat, that He may know to refuse evil, and choose good.

You are gods; in fact, all of you are children of the most High. He shall build an house for My Name, and I will establish the throne of His kingdom for ever. I will be His Father, and He shall be My Son. I set my King on My holy hill. I will declare the decree: the LORD has said to Me, You are My Son; this day I have begotten You. For unto us a Child is born, a Son is given: the government shall be on His shoulder: His Name shall be called Wonderful, Counsellor,

The mighty God, The everlasting Father, The Prince of Peace. His government shall prevail and there shall be no end of peace, on the throne of David, and His kingdom, to order it, and to establish it with justice and righteousness from henceforth, even for ever.

When John sees many of the Pharisees and Sadducees come to his baptism, he says to them, Bring forth fruits in keeping with repentance: Do not think to say within yourselves, We have Abraham as our father: for I say to you, God is able to raise up children of Abraham from these stones. Now the axe lies at the root of the trees: every tree which brings not forth good fruit is hewn down, and cast into the fire. I baptise you with water unto repentance: but He who comes after me is mightier than I. He shall baptise you with the Holy Spirit, and with fire: whose fan is in His hand, and He will thoroughly purge His floor, and gather His wheat into the barn; but He will burn up the chaff with unquenchable fire.

The devil says to Him, If You are the Son of God, command this stone into bread. Jesus answers him, it is written, Man shall not live by bread alone, but by every word of God. He brings Him to Jerusalem, set Him on a pinnacle of the temple, and says, If You are the Son of God, jump down from here: For it is written, He shall give His angels charge over You, to keep You and their hands shall bear You up, lest at any time You dash Your foot against a stone. Jesus answers him, it says, You shall not tempt the Lord your God.

He goes into the synagogue on the sabbath day, and stand up to read from the book of the prophet Isaiah where it is written, The Spirit of the Lord is on Me, and anointed Me to preach the gospel to the poor; He sends Me to heal the brokenhearted, to preach deliverance to the bound, restore sight to the blind, to set free those who are bruised, to preach the year of the Lord's favour. The time is now and God's kingdom is near, you therefore, repent and believe the euangelion (good news) of Messiah Jesus, the Son of God.

One Who Has Authority (1:16-31)

As He walked by the sea of Galilee, He saw Simon and Andrew his brother casting a net into the sea: for they were fishermen. Jesus says to them, Come after Me, and I will make you fishers of men. Straightaway they forsook their nets, and followed Him. When He had gone a little further, He saw James the son of Zebedee, and John his brother, who were in the boat mending nets. Straightaway He called them and they left their father Zebedee in the boat with the hired servants, and went after Him. They went to Capernaum and straightaway on the sabbath day He entered into the synagogue, and taught. They were astonished at His teaching: for He taught them as one who has authority, and not as the scribes. In their synagogue was a man with an unclean spirit; and he cries out, saying, Let us alone; what have we to do with You, Jesus of Nazareth? Have You come to destroy us? I know who You are, the Holy One of God. Jesus rebuked him, saying, Hold your peace, and come out of him. When the unclean spirit had torn him and cried with a loud voice, he came out of him. They were all amazed that they questioned among themselves, saying, What thing is this? What new teaching is this? For with authority He commands even the unclean spirits, and they obey Him. Immediately His fame spread abroad throughout all the region round about Galilee. When they went out of the synagogue, they entered into Simon's house with Andrew, James and John. Simon's wife's mother lay sick of a fever, and they tell Him of her. He came, took her by the hand, lifted her up; immediately the fever left her, and she ministered to them.

As the people presses upon Him to hear the word of God, He stands by the lake of Gennesaret, and sees two boats by the lake but the fishermen have gone out of them, and are washing their nets. He enters into one of the boats, belonging to Simon and ask him to thrust out a little from shore. He sits down and teach the people out of the boat. When He is done speaking, He says to Simon, Launch out into the deep, and let down your net for a catch. Simon answering Him, says, Master, we toil all night and caught nothing: nevertheless at Your word I will let down the net. When they did this, they enclosed a great multitude of fishes until their net is breaking. They beckon to their partners in the other boat to come and help them. They come and fill both boats until they begin to sink. When Simon Peter saw it, he falls down at Jesus' knees, saying, Depart from me; O Master, for I am a sinful man. He is astonished at the catch of the fishes, so also James and John, the sons of Zebedee, who are partners with Simon. Jesus says to Simon, Fear not; from now on, you shall catch men. When they bring their boats to shore, forsaking all, they followed Him.

Leaving Nazareth, He comes and dwell in Capernaum, which is upon the sea coast, on the borders of Zabulon and Nephthalim: fulfilling what was spoken by the prophet Isaiah, saying, The land of Zabulon and Nephthalim, by the way of the sea, beyond Jordan, Galilee of the nations: the people who sits in darkness sees a great light; and to them who sits in the region and shadow of death, light springs up. From that time on, Jesus begin to preach, and to say, Repent: for the kingdom of heaven is at hand.

He comes to Capernaum of Galilee, teaching on the sabbath days. They are astonished at His teaching: for His word is with authority. A man in the synagogue having a spirit of an unclean devil, cries out with a loud voice, Let us alone; what have we to do with You, Jesus of Nazareth? Have You come to destroy us? I know who You are; the Holy One of God. Jesus rebukes him, saying, Hold your peace, and come out of him. When the devil throws him down, he come out and did not hurt him. They are all amazed, speaking among themselves, saying, What a word this is! For with authority and power He commands the unclean spirits, and they come out.

What is this thing? What new teaching? What a word this is! A multitude of fishes caught and unclean spirits come out at His Word. Like Peter, the only apt respond to Jesus is simply confess: O Master, I am a sinful person; and hear Him say, Fear not, from now on, catch people. Forsake all and follow Him. Simply obey. Word.

Everyone Seek for You (1:32-45)

When the sun set, they brought to Him all who were diseased and possessed with devils. All the city gathered at the door. He healed many sick of diverse diseases, cast out many devils; and permitted not the devils to speak, because they knew Him. In the morning, rising up very early before daybreak, He departed into a solitary place to pray. Simon and the others followed after Him. When they found Him, say, Everyone seek for You. He says to them, Let us go to the next towns, that I may preach there also: for this purpose I came. He preached in the synagogues throughout Galilee, and cast out devils. There came a leper, beseeching Him, and kneeling down, and say to Him, If You will, You can make me clean. Jesus, moved with compassion, put forth His hand, touched him, and says to him, I will; be clean. As soon as He had spoken, immediately the leprosy departed from him, and he was cleansed. He strictly charged him, and sent him away; and says to him, Say nothing to any one: but go your way, show yourself to the priest, and offer for your cleansing those things which Moses commanded, for a testimony to them. But he went out, and began to publish it much, blaze abroad the matter, until Jesus could no more openly enter into the city, but was outside in desert places: and they came to Him from every quarter.

Now when the sun sets, those sick with diverse diseases are brought to Him; He lay His hands on every one and heal them. Devils come out of many, crying out, and saying, You are Messiah, the Son of God. He rebukes them, did not permit them to speak: for they know He is Messiah. When it was daybreak, He leaves and goes to a desert place to pray. People seek Him, and come to Him, and hold Him back, that He should not leave them. He says to them, I must preach the kingdom of God to other cities also: for therefore am I sent. And He preaches in the synagogues of Galilee.

When He is in a certain city, behold a man full of leprosy: who, seeing Jesus, falls on his face, and beg Him, saying, Master, if You will, You can make me clean. He puts forth His hand, and touch him, saying, I will: be clean. Immediately the leprosy leave him. He charge him to tell no one: Go and show yourself to the priest, and offer for your cleansing, according as Moses commanded, for a testimony to them. But all the more His fame goes abroad and a great multitude come together to hear Him, and be healed of their infirmities. He withdrew Himself into the wilderness to pray.

When Jesus enters Capernaum, there come to Him a centurion, begging Him, saying, Master, my servant lies at home a paraplegic, grievously tormented. Jesus says to him, I will come and heal him. The centurion answer and says, Master, I am not worthy that You come under my roof: but speak the word only, and my servant shall be healed. For I am a man under authority, having soldiers under me: and I say to this man, Go, and he goes; and to another, Come, and he comes; and to my servant, Do this, and he does it. When Jesus heard it, He marvel and says to them that follow, Truly I say to you, I have not found so great faith, no, not in Israel. And I say to you, That many shall come from the east and west, and shall sit down with Abraham, and Isaac, and Jacob, in the kingdom of heaven. But the children of the kingdom shall be cast out into outer darkness: where there shall be weeping and gnashing of teeth. Jesus says to the centurion, Go your way; as you believe, so be it done to you. His servant was healed in the same hour.

Everyone seek for Jesus. Moved with compassion, He heals all who seek Him of diverse diseases, unclean evil spirits and infirmities. Then He goes out to a solitary place to pray. Everyone seek for Jesus. What about you? Do you seek for Him? Do you hear Him calling you? He will not linger to wait for you and He will move on to call others. A non-Jewish army captain surprises Him by saying, Speak the word only; believing his servant will be healed because he recognises Jesus' power and authority. Many people come seeking Him for cleansing, healing and deliverance but He come seeking those with faith who believe in Him and repent.

Who Can Forgive Sins But God Only (2:1-13)

He entered Capernaum after some days; and they heard He was in the house. Straightaway many gathered, until there was no room to receive them, packed up to the door: and He preached the word to them. They come to Him, bringing a paraplegic, carried by four people. When they could not come near Him due to the crowd, they uncovered the roof where He was: and when they had broken it up, they let down the bed where the paraplegic lay. When Jesus saw their faith, He says to the paraplegic, Son, your sins are forgiven. Certain scribes sitting there, reasoned in their hearts, Why does this man speak blasphemies? Who can forgive sins but God only? When Jesus perceived in His spirit they so reasoned within themselves, He says, Why reason these things in your hearts? Which is easier to say to the paraplegic, Your sins are forgiven you; or to say, Arise, and take up your bed, and walk? But that you may know the Son of Man has authority on earth to forgive sins, (He says to the paraplegic,) I say to you, Arise, and take up your bed, and go your way into your house. Immediately he arose, took up the bed, and went forth before them all; until they were all amazed, and glorified God, saying, We have never seen anything like this. He went again by the seaside; and the multitude come to Him, and He taught them.

Is it easier, to say, Your sins are forgiven you; or to say, Rise up and walk? But that you may know that the Son of Man has authority on earth to forgive sins, (He says to the paraplegic,) I say to you, Arise, and take up your bed, and go to your house. Immediately he rises up before them, takes up his bed, and goes to his own house, glorifying God. They are all amazed and glorify God, and with fear, say, We have seen strange things today.

So what strange things have they seen that cause them to be amazed and glorify God while filled with fear at the same time? It is one thing to claim one has power to heal and prove his ability by healing someone or deliver them from devils as people can see and the ones restored can testify. It is another to claim both the ability to heal diseases and the authority to forgive sins at the same time.

People instinctively know that God alone can forgive sin. So when Jesus springs a surprise by saying to the paraplegic: Son, your sins are forgiven, they concluded logically that Jesus is blaspheming by claiming He could forgive sins. On the other hand, would it not also be logical, supposing if He was indeed deluded or lying, that God would have prevented and disallowed the healing if Jesus was not telling the truth? Surely God would have stopped it.

It would be reasonable to expect the opposite outcome, after making such an extraordinary and outrageous statement, that the paraplegic remains unhealed and exposed Jesus to be blasphemous as the scribes had thought. Instead, they were proven to be mistaken and Jesus' claims were irrefutable.

The Son of Man's authority on earth to forgive sins was confirmed by the healing of the paraplegic after He says to him first of all that his sins are forgiven, and then commanding him to take up his bed and go home, for straightaway he stands up, picks up his bed and goes home. No one has seen anything like it.

Another strange thing is the way Jesus calls the paraplegic, son. It is clear He meant it to not as a literal relationship between them as we see later in the next chapter His saying that anyone who does God's will is His brother, sister and mother. He calls him son to restore his relationship back with God the Father as joint-heirs.

The people saw something wonderfully strange that day. Jesus has power to not only heal the sick, cast out devils, but authority on earth to forgive sin. They are filled with awe and joy but also with fear and hope of restoring a right relationship with God the Father as sons and daughters of God through Jesus the Son.

As many as received Him, He gave authority to become the children of God, to those who believe on His Name: who were born, not of blood, nor the will of the flesh, nor of the will of man, but of God.

New Wine Must Be Put Into New Wineskin (2:14-28)

As He passed by, he saw Levi the son of Alphaeus sitting at the receipt of custom, and say to him, Follow Me. He arose and followed Him. As Jesus sat at meat in his house, many tax collectors and sinners sat together with Jesus and His disciples: for there were many who followed Him. When the scribes and Pharisees saw Him eat with tax collectors and sinners, they say to His disciples, How is it that He eats and drinks with tax collectors and sinners? When Jesus heard it, He says to them, Those who are whole have no need of the physician, but those who are sick: I came not to call the righteous, but sinners to repentance. John's disciples and the Pharisees' used to fast: and they come and say to Him, Why do John's disciples and the Pharisees' fast, but Your disciples fast not? Jesus says to them, Can the children of the bridechamber fast, while the bridegroom is with them? As long the bridegroom is with them, they cannot fast. The days will come, when the bridegroom is taken away, then shall they fast in those days. No one sews a piece of new cloth on an old garment: else the new piece tears away from the old, and the rent is made worse. No one puts new wine into old wineskins: else the new wine burst the wineskin, and the wine is spilled, and the wineskin will be ruined: but new wine must be put into new wineskin. He went through the corn fields on the sabbath day; and His disciples began to pluck the ears of corn. The Pharisees say to Him, Behold, why do they on the sabbath day that which is not lawful? He says to them, Have you not read what David did, when he had need, and was hungry, he and those with him? How he went into the house of God in the days of Abiathar the high priest, and eat the showbread, which is not lawful to eat but for the priests, and gave also to those with him? He says to them, The sabbath was made for mankind, and not mankind for the sabbath: Therefore the Son of Man is Lord also of the sabbath.

When the Pharisees saw it, they say to His disciples, Why does your Master eat with tax collectors and sinners? When Jesus heard that, He says to them, Those who are whole need not a physician, but those who are sick. But go and learn what this means, I will have mercy, and not sacrifice: for I am not come to call the righteous, but sinners to repentance. Then the disciples of John came to Him, saying, Why do we and the Pharisees fast often, but Your disciples fast not? Jesus says to them, Can the children of the bridechamber mourn, as long as the bridegroom is with them? The days will come, when the bridegroom is taken from them, then shall they fast. No one puts a piece of new cloth on an old garment, for what is put in to fill it up takes from the garment, and the rent is made worse. Neither do one put new wine into old wineskin: or else the wineskin breaks, and the wine runs out, and the wineskin perish: but they put new wine into new wineskin, and both are preserved. No one having drunk old wine straightaway desire new: for he or she says, The old is better. It takes time get use to new.

Certain Pharisees say to them, Why do you that which is not lawful on the sabbath days? Jesus answering them says, Have you not read this, what David did, when he was hungry and those who were with him; How he went into the house of God and took and ate the showbread, and gave to those who were with him; which it is not lawful to eat but for the priests alone?

Or have you not read in the law, how that on the sabbath days the priests in the temple broke the sabbath, and were blameless? But I say to you, That in this place is one greater than the temple. But if you know what this means, I will have mercy, and not sacrifice, you would not condemn the guiltless. For the Son of Man is Lord even of the sabbath day. For I desire mercy, and not sacrifice; and the knowledge of God more than burnt offerings.

Show us Your mercy, O Lord, and grant us Your deliverance. I will hear what God the Lord will speak: for He will speak peace to His people, and to His saints: but let them not turn again to folly. Surely His deliverance is near those who fear Him; that glory may dwell in our land. Mercy and truth are met together; righteousness and peace kiss each other. He or she shall have judgment without mercy who shows no mercy; and mercy rejoices against judgment.

Is it Lawful to Do Good on Sabbath? (3:1-19)

He entered the synagogue, and there was a man with a withered hand. They watched Him to see if He would heal on the sabbath day; to accuse Him. He says to the man with the withered hand, Stand forth. He says to them, Is it lawful to do good on the sabbath days, or to do evil? To save life, or to kill? They held their peace. He looked round about on them with anger, grieved for their hardness of hearts, He says to the man, Stretch forth your hand. He stretched it out: and his hand was restored whole as the other. The Pharisees went and straightaway took counsel with the Herodians against Him, how they might destroy Him. Jesus withdrew Himself with His disciples to the sea: and a great multitude from Galilee followed Him. From Judaea, Jerusalem, Idumaea, beyond Jordan; Tyre and Sidon, a great multitude, when they heard what great things He did, came to Him. He spoke to His disciples, that a small boat should wait on Him because of the multitude, lest they should throng Him. For He had healed many; until they pressed upon Him to touch Him, as many as had plagues. Unclean spirits, when they saw Him, fell down before Him, and cried, saying, You are the Son of God. He strictly charged them they should not make Him known. He goes up into a mountain, calls to Him whom He would: and they came to Him. He appoints twelve to be with Him, send them forth to preach, give authority to heal sicknesses, and to cast out devils. Simon, He surnamed Peter; James the son of Zebedee and John his brother, He surnamed them Boanerges, which is, The sons of thunder. Andrew and Philip, Bartholomew and Matthew, Thomas and James the son of Alphaeus, Thaddaeus and Simon the Canaanite, and Judas Iscariot, who also betrayed Him: and they went into a house.

On another sabbath, He enters the synagogue to teach: and there is a man whose right hand is withered. The scribes and Pharisees watch Him to see if He would heal on the sabbath day in order to find an accusation against Him. He knew their thoughts, and says to the man with the withered hand, Rise up, and stand forth in the midst. And he arises and stood forth. Jesus says to them, I will ask you one thing; Is it lawful on the sabbath days to do good, or to do evil? To save life, or to destroy it? And looking round about on them all, He says to the man, Stretch forth your hand. And he did so: and his hand is restored whole as the other. Raging with madness, they discussed with each other what to do to Jesus.

These twelve Jesus sends forth, and command them, saying, Go not in the nations' way, nor enter any city of the Samaritans. Go rather to the lost sheep of the house of Israel. As you go, preach, saying, The kingdom of heaven is at hand. Heal the sick, cleanse the lepers, raise the dead, cast out devils: freely you have received, freely give. Provide neither gold or silver, nor money in your purses or food pouches for your journey, neither two coats, sandals, nor even a walking stick: for the worker is worthy to be cared for. Whatever city or town you enter, enquire who in it is worthy; and remain there till you leave the place. When you come into a house, salute it. And if the house be worthy, let your peace come upon it: but if it be not worthy, let your peace return to you. Whoever shall not receive you, nor hear your words, when you depart out of that house or city, shake off the dust of your feet. Truly I say to you, it shall be more tolerable for Sodom and Gomorrah in the day of judgment than for that city. Behold, I send you forth as sheep in the midst of wolves: therefore be wise as serpents, harmless as doves.

Behold, you fast to contend and quarrel, to strike with the fist of wickedness: you shall not fast as you do this day to make your voice heard on high. Is this a fast I have chosen? A day for one to afflict their soul? Bow one's head as a reed, to spread sackcloth and ashes under them? Will you call this a fast an acceptable day to the Lord? Is not this the fast I have chosen? To loose the chains of wickedness, undo heavy burdens, let the oppressed go free and break every bond? Is it not to feed the hungry and bring the poor outcast to your house? When you see the naked, you cover up; and you hide not yourself from your own flesh? Do not keep rituals and ignore the poor, or fail to do good to the needy, nor call good evil.

Can Satan Cast Out Satan? (3:20-35)

The multitude come together again, until they could not eat bread. When His friends heard of it, they went out to lay hold on Him: for they said, He is mad. The scribes who came down from Jerusalem said, He has Beelzebub, and by the prince of the devils cast out devils. He calls them to Him, and say to them in parables, How can Satan cast out Satan? If a kingdom is divided against itself, that kingdom cannot stand. If a house is divided against itself, that house cannot stand. If Satan rise up against himself, and is divided, he cannot stand, but has an end. No one can enter into a strong man's house, and spoil his goods, except one first bind the strong man; then one will spoil his house. Truly I say to you, All sins shall be forgiven the children of men, and blasphemies where they blaspheme: But one who blaspheme against the Holy Spirit has no forgiveness, but is in danger of eternal damnation: because they said, He has an unclean spirit. There came His brothers and mother, standing outside, sent to Him, calling Him. The multitude sat about Him, and say to Him, Behold, your mother and brothers outside seek for You He answered them, saying, Who is My mother, or My brothers? He looked round about them who sat about Him, and says, Behold My mother and My brothers! For anyone who does the will of God, the same is My brother, and My sister, and mother.

As they went out, behold, they brought to Him a dumb man possessed with a devil. And when the devil is cast out, the dumb speaks: and the multitude marvel, saying, It is never so seen in Israel before. The Pharisees say, He cast out devils through the prince of the devils. Jesus goes about all the cities and villages, teaching in their synagogues, preaching the gospel of the kingdom, healing every sickness and every disease among the people. When He sees the multitude, He is moved with compassion, because they faint and are scattered abroad, as sheep having no Shepherd.

The disciple is not above his master, nor the servant his lord. It is enough for the disciple to be as his master, the servant as his lord. If they called the master of the house Beelzebub, how much more shall they call them of his household? Fear not: for there is nothing covered, that shall not be exposed; and hid, that shall not be revealed. What I tell you in darkness, speak in the light and what you hear in the ear, preach upon the housetops. Fear not those who kill the body, but are not able to kill the soul: rather, fear Him who is able to destroy both soul and body in hell. Are not two sparrows sold for a penny? One of them shall not fall on the ground without your Father. The very hairs of your head are all numbered. Fear not, you are of more value than many sparrows. Whoever confess Me before people, him or her will I confess before My Father in heaven. Whoever deny Me before people, him or her will I deny before My Father in heaven. Think not I am come to send peace on earth: I come not to send peace, but a sword. For I am come to set a man at odds against his father, and the daughter against her mother, and the daughter in law against her mother in law. And a man's foes shall be his own household. One who loves father or mother more than Me is not worthy of Me: and one who loves son or daughter more than Me is not worthy of Me. And one who takes not the cross, and follows after Me, is not worthy of Me. He who finds his life shall lose it: and she who loses her life for My sake shall find it.

Every kingdom divided against itself ends in desolation, a house divided against itself falls. If Satan divides against himself, how shall his kingdom stand? Because you say that I cast out devils through Beelzebub. If I by Beelzebub cast out devils, by whom do your children cast out? Therefore they are your judges. If I with God's finger cast out devils, no doubt God's kingdom is upon you.

Why call Me Lord, Lord, but do not what I say? Not every one who says to Me, Lord, Lord, shall enter into the kingdom of heaven; but he or she who does the will of My Father in heaven. The one who does God's will is My brother, and My sister and mother.

One Who Has Ears, Let One Hear (4:1-20)

He began to teach by the seaside: and there was gathered a great multitude, so He entered a boat by the sea; and the multitude was on land. He taught many things by parables, and says in His teaching, Hearken; Behold, there went out a sower to sow: as he sowed, some fell by the wayside, and the birds of the air came and devoured it up. Some fell on stony ground, where it had not much earth; immediately it sprang up, because it had no depth of earth. But when the sun was up, it was scorched; and because it had no root, it withered away. Some fell among thorns, and the thorns grew up, and choked it, yielding no fruit. Others fell on good ground, and yield fruit that sprang up and increased; brought forth some thirty, some sixty, some an hundred. He says to them, One who has ears to hear, let one hear. When He was alone, those with the twelve asked Him the parable. He says to them, To you it is given to know the mystery of the kingdom of God: but to outsiders, all these things are done in parables: That seeing they may see, and not perceive; and hearing they may hear, and not understand; lest at any time they should turn, and their sins should be forgiven them. He says to them, Know you not this parable? How then will you know all parables? The sower sows the word. These are they by the wayside, where the word is sown; but when they have heard, Satan comes immediately, and takes away the word that was sown in their hearts. Likewise, these are they which are sown on stony ground; who, when they have heard the word, immediately receive it with gladness; and have no root in themselves, and so endure for a time: afterward, when affliction or persecution arises for the word's sake, immediately they are offended. These are they which are sown among thorns; such as hear the word, and the cares of this world, the deceitfulness of riches, and the lusts of other things entering in, choke the word, and it becomes unfruitful. These are they which are sown on good ground; such as hear the word, and receive it, and bring forth fruit, some thirtyfold, some sixty, some an hundred.

The disciples say to Him, Why do You speak with them in parables? He answers and say to them, Because it is given you to know the mysteries of the kingdom of heaven, but to them it is not given. Whoever has, shall be given and he or she shall have more abundance: whoever has not, even what one has shall be taken away. I speak to them in parables: because seeing, they see not; and hearing, they hear not, neither do they understand. In them the prophecy of Isaiah is fulfilled, which says, By hearing you shall hear and not understand; and seeing you shall see and not perceive. For this people's heart is wax gross, their ears are dull of hearing, they close their eyes; lest at any time they see with their eyes, hear with their ears, and understand with their heart, and turn, and I heal them. Blessed are your eyes, for they see: and your ears, for they hear. Truly I say to you, many prophets and righteous ones desired to see those things which you see, but have not seen; and to hear those things which you hear, and have not heard. Now the parable is this: The seed is the word of God. Those by the wayside are those who hear; then comes the devil, and takes away the word out of their hearts, lest they believe and are delivered. Those on the rock are those who, when they hear, receive the word with joy; and these having no root for a while believe, and in time of temptation fall away. Those which fell among thorns are those who, when they hear, go forth and are choked with cares, riches and pleasures of this life, and bring no fruit to perfection. Those on good ground are those who, in an noble and good heart, hear the word, keep it, and bring forth fruit with patience. Jesus spoke to the multitude in parables; without a parable He spoke not to them, fulfilling what the prophet spoke, I will open my mouth in parables; I will utter things kept secret from the foundation of the world. Let the one who has ears to hear, hears what the Spirit is saying to him or her.

Be doers of the word, and not hearers only, deceiving your own self. If any one is a hearer of the word and not a doer, it is like one beholding one's natural face in a mirror: seeing oneself, goes away, and straightaway forget what kind of person he or she is. Being not a forgetful hearer, but a doer of good works, one shall be blessed.

The Wind and the Sea Obey Him (4:21-41)

He says to them, Is a candle put under a bushel, or under a bed and not set on a candlestick? Everything hidden shall be revealed; anything secret shall be exposed. If any one have ears to hear, let him or her hear. He says to them, Take heed what you hear: the measure you mete shall be measured to you: and to you who hear shall more be given. One who has shall be given; one who has not, even what one has shall be taken. He says, So is God's kingdom, as if one cast seed into the ground and sleep, rises night and day, the seed spring and grow up, one knows not how. For the earth brings forth fruit of herself; first the blade, then the ear, then the full corn in the ear. When the fruit is brought forth, immediately one puts in the sickle, because the harvest is come. He says, How shall we liken God's kingdom? Or what shall we compare it to? It is like a grain of mustard seed, when it is sown in the earth, is less than all the seeds in the earth. But when sown, it grows up, becomes greater than all herbs, shoots out great branches; so the birds of the air may lodge under the shadow of it. With many such parables He spoke the word to them, as they were able to hear it. He did not speak without a parable to them and when they were alone, He expounded all things to His disciples. When evening comes, He says, Let us pass over to the other side. When they had sent away the multitude, they took Him in the boat. There were other little boats. There arose a great stormy wind, and the waves beat into the boat, so that it was now full. He was in the back of the boat, asleep on a pillow: and they woke Him, and say to Him, Master, do You not care that we perish? He arose, and rebuked the wind, and says to the sea, Peace, be still. And the wind ceased, and there was a great calm. He says to them, Why are you so fearful? How is it that you have no faith? They feared exceedingly, and said one to another, What manner of man is this, that even the wind and the sea obey Him?

No one light a candle, cover it with a vessel, or put it under a bed but set it on a candlestick, that those who enter in may see the light. For nothing is secret, that shall not be exposed; neither any thing hid, that shall not be known and become clear. Take heed therefore how you hear: for whoever has, to one shall be given; and whoever has not, from one shall be taken even what one has.

The kingdom of heaven is like a man who sows good seed in his field: While men sleeps, his enemy comes and sow weeds among the wheat, and goes his way. When the blade springs up and brings forth fruit, then the weeds appear also. The servants of the householder come and say to him, Sir, did you not sow good seed in your field? Why then has it weeds? He says to them, An enemy has done this. The servants say to him, Shall we go and gather them up? No; lest while you gather up the weeds, you root up also the wheat with them. Let both grow together until harvest time when I will tell the reapers, Gather together first the weeds, bind them to burn them: but gather the wheat into my barn.

He who sows good seed is the Son of Man; The field is the world; the good seed are the children of the kingdom; the weeds are the children of the wicked one. The enemy who sow them is the devil; the harvest is the end of the age; and the reapers are the angels. As the weeds are gathered and burned in the fire; so shall it be in the end of this age. The Son of Man sends forth His angels, and they shall gather out of His kingdom all things that offend, and those who do lawlessness; and cast them into a furnace of fire: there shall be wailing and gnashing of teeth. Then shall the righteous shine forth as the sun in the kingdom of their Father.

On a certain day, He goes into a boat with His disciples and says to them, Let us go over to the other side of the lake. They launch forth. As they sail, He falls asleep and a stormy wind comes down on the lake; and they are filled with water, and are in jeopardy. They come and wake Him, saying, Master, Master, we perish. Then He rises and rebuke the wind and the raging of the water: they ceased and there is a calm. He says to them, Where is your faith? Being afraid, they wonder, and say to each other, What manner of man is this! for He commands even the winds and water, and they obey Him. Who is He? Jesus has power even over the forces of nature.

Jesus, Son of the Most High God (5:1-20)

They came to the other side into the country of the Gadarenes. When He comes out of the boat, immediately there met Him out of the tombs a man with an unclean spirit, who live among the tombs; and no man could bind him. He had often been bound with fetters and chains, and he would break them in pieces: nor could any one tame him. Always, night and day, he was in the mountains and the tombs, crying and cutting himself with stones. When he saw Jesus afar off, he ran and worshipped Him, and cries with a loud voice, and say, What have I to do with You, Jesus, Son of the most high God? I adjure You by God, that You torment me not. For He says to him, Come out of the man, you unclean spirit. He asks him, What is your name? He answers, saying, My name is Legion: for we are many. He begged Him much that He would not send them out of the country. Near the mountains, a great herd of pigs is feeding. All the devils begged Him, saying, Send us into the pigs, that we may enter into them. Jesus gave them leave. All the unclean spirits entered into the pigs: and the herd ran violently down a steep place into the sea, (they were about two thousand;) and drowned. They that fed the pigs fled, and told it in the city, and the country. They went out to see how it happened. They came to Jesus, and saw him that was possessed with the devil, and had the legion, sitting and clothed, in his right mind and they were afraid. They that saw told them how it befell him that was possessed with the devil, and also concerning the pigs. They pleaded with Him to depart out of their coasts. When He comes into the boat, he that had been possessed with the devil pleaded with Him to be with Him. Jesus did not permit him, but says to him, Go home to your friends, tell them what great things the Master has done for you, and has had compassion on you. He departed and began to publish in Decapolis what great things Jesus had done for him: and all people did marvel.

They arrived at the country of the Gadarenes, which is over against Galilee. When He goes forth to land, there met Him out of the city a certain man, who had devils long time, and wore no clothes, neither lived in any house, but in the tombs. When he sees Jesus, he cries out and falls down before Him, and with a loud voice says, What have I to do with You, Jesus, Son of God most high?

The devils recognised Jesus is the Son of the most high God, and entreated Him not to torment them but to send them into a herd of pigs which ran into a lake and drowned. The people there, seeing how He healed the man possessed by devils, reacted with great fear, and beg Him to leave their country. They were both afraid and felt more sorry for the loss of pigs than they were glad of the healing and deliverance of a fellow villager who lives naked among the tombs possessed by a legion of devils. Obviously, they had their priorities upside down and promptly rejected Jesus by telling Him to go back to where He came from. The man who had a legion of devils and was healed, clothed and in his right mind, however, begs Jesus to take him along. Jesus declined and tells him to go home to his friends and tell them what great things the Master has done for him and has compassion on him.

In the sixth month the angel Gabriel, sent from God to a city of Galilee, named Nazareth, to a virgin engaged to a man whose name is Joseph of the house of David; and the virgin's name is Mary. The angel comes to her, and say, Hail, you are highly favoured, the Lord is with you: blessed are you among women. When she sees him, she was troubled at his saying, and ponder what manner of salutation this is. The angel says to her, Fear not, Mary: for you have found favour with God. Behold, you shall conceive in your womb, and bring forth a Son, and shall call His Name JESUS. He shall be great, and shall be called the Son of the Highest: and the Lord God shall give to Him the throne of His father David. He shall reign over the house of Jacob for ever; and of His kingdom there shall be no end.

But love your enemies, do good, and lend, hoping for nothing in return again; and your reward shall be great, and you shall be the children of the Highest: for He is kind to the unthankful and to the evil. Be therefore merciful, as your Father also is merciful. We are sons and daughters of the most high God when we act like Him.

Your Faith Has Made You Whole (5:21-43)

When Jesus passed over again by boat to the other side, many people gathered to Him: and He was near the sea. Behold, there comes one of the synagogue rulers, Jairus by name; and when he saw Him, fell at His feet, and begged Him greatly, saying, My little daughter lies at the point of death: Please come and lay Your hands on her, that she may be healed and live. Jesus went with him; and many people followed and thronged Him. A certain woman, who had an issue of blood twelve years, suffered many things of many physicians, spent all she had and nothing bettered, but grew worse, When she heard of Jesus, came from behind, and touched His garment. She says, If I may touch but His clothes, I shall be whole. Straightaway the fountain of her blood dried up; and she felt in her body she was healed of that plague. Jesus, immediately knowing in Himself that virtue had gone out of Him, turned about and says, Who touched My clothes? His disciples say to Him, You see the multitude thronging You and You say, Who touched Me? He looked round about to see her who had done this thing. The woman fearing and trembling, knowing what was done in her, came and fell down before Him, and told Him all the truth. He says to her, Daughter, your faith has made you whole; go in peace, and be whole of your plague. As He spoke, there came from the synagogue's ruler house certain ones who said, Your daughter is dead: why trouble the Master any further? As soon as Jesus heard the word that was spoken, He says to the synagogue's ruler, Be not afraid, only believe. He permitted no one to follow Him, except Peter, James and John the brother of James. He comes to the house of the synagogue's ruler, and sees the tumult, and those who wept and wailed greatly. When He comes in, He says to them, Why are you weeping? The damsel is not dead, but sleeps. They laughed Him to scorn. When He had put them all out, He takes the father and the mother of the damsel, and those with Him, and enters in where the damsel was lying. He took the damsel by the hand, and says to her, Talitha cumi; which is, being interpreted, Little girl, I say to you, get up. And straightaway the little girl arose, and walked; for she was twelve years old. And they were astonished with a great astonishment. And He charged them strictly that no one should know it; and commanded that something should be given her to eat.

A man named Jairus, a ruler of the synagogue, falls down at Jesus' feet and begs Him to come to his house to save his only daughter about twelve years of age, as she lays dying. A woman, having an issue of blood twelve years, spent all her savings on physicians, yet found no cure, comes behind Him and touch the border of His garment: immediately her issue of blood stops. Jesus says, Who touched Me? When all denied it, Peter and those with Him says, Master, the multitude throng and presses You, and You say, Who touched Me? Jesus says, Someone touched Me: for I perceive that virtue is gone out of Me. When the woman saw that she could not hide, came trembling, falls down and declares to Him before all the people for what cause she touched Him, and how she is healed immediately. He says to her, Daughter, be of good comfort: your faith has made you whole; go in peace. As He speaks, one from the synagogue's ruler house, says to him, Your daughter is dead; trouble not the Master. When Jesus heard it, He answers him, saying, Fear not: only believe, she shall be made whole. When He comes into the house, He permitted no one to go in, except Peter, James and John, the father and mother of the maiden. All wept and bewailed her, but He says, Weep not; she is not dead, but sleeps. They laughed Him to scorn, since she is dead. He puts them all out, takes her by the hand, and call, saying, Little girl, arise. Her spirit comes again, straightaway she arose: He commands to give her meat. Her parents are astonished: but He charge them to tell no one.

The woman was healed of her physical condition when she touched Jesus' garment, but her declaration and faith made her emotionally and psychologically whole as well when she testifies openly before a crowd around her what Jesus had done for her. Yet, He charged Jairus to tell no one He raised his daughter from the dead. To get a touch from Jesus is so real. Fear not, only believe and you shall be made whole in body and mind, spirit and soul.

Prophet Without Honour in His Own House (6:1-29)

He came to His own country; and His disciples follow Him. When the sabbath day comes, He began to teach in the synagogue. Many hearing Him were astonished, saying, From where has this man these things? What wisdom is this given Him, that such mighty works are wrought by His hands? Is not this the carpenter, son of Mary, brother of James, Joses, Judas, and Simon? Are not His sisters here with us? They were offended at Him. Jesus says to them, A prophet is without honour in His own country, among His own kin, and in His own house. He could do no mighty work except to lay His hands on a few sick folk and healed them. He marvelled because of their unbelief. He went about the villages, teaching. He called the twelve and began to send them forth two by two; gave them authority over unclean spirits; and commanded them to take nothing for their journey, save a staff only; no pouch, no bread, no money in their purse, shod with sandals; and not put on two coats. He says to them, In what place you enter into a house, there abide till you depart from that place. Whoever shall not receive you, nor hear you, when you depart, shake off the dust under your feet for a testimony against them. Truly I say to you, It shall be more tolerable for Sodom and Gomorrah in the day of judgment than for that city. They went and preached that people should repent, cast out many devils, anointed with oil many sick and healed them. King Herod heard of Him; (for His Name was spread abroad) and he said, John the Baptist is risen from the dead, therefore mighty works show forth themselves in Him. Others said, It is Elias or one of the prophets. When Herod heard, he said, It is John, whom I beheaded: he is risen from the dead. Herod himself laid hold of John, bound him in prison for Herodias' sake, his brother Philip's wife: for he had married her. John said to Herod, It is not lawful for you to have your brother's wife. Therefore Herodias had a quarrel against him, and would have killed him; but she could not. Herod feared John, knowing he was a righteous and holy man, and observed him; when he heard he did many things, heard him gladly. When it was his birthday, Herod made a feast for his officials, military top brass, and prominent leaders of Galilee. The daughter of Herodias came in and danced, pleasing Herod and those who sat with him. The king says to the damsel, Ask me anything, and I will give you. He swore to her, I will give even half of my kingdom. She went to her mother, What shall I ask? She says, The head of John the Baptist. She came in straightaway with haste to the king, and ask, saying, I want the head of John the Baptist on a platter. The king was exceeding sorry; yet for his oath's sake, and for their sakes who sat with him, he would not reject her. Immediately the king sent an executioner, commanded his head to be brought: and he went and beheaded him in the prison, brought his head on a platter, gave it to the damsel: and the damsel gave it to her mother. When his disciples heard of it, they came and took up his corpse, and laid it in a tomb.

He came to His own country and taught them in their synagogue. They are astonished, and says, Where has this man this wisdom, and these mighty works? Is not this the carpenter's son? Why has this man all these things? And they are offended by Him. Jesus says to them, A prophet is not without honour, except in his own country and in his own house. He did not do many mighty works there because of their unbelief.

He called His twelve disciples together, gave them power and authority over all devils, and to cure diseases. He sends them to preach the kingdom of God and to heal the sick, Whichever house you enter, remain there until you leave. Whoever will not receive you, when you go out of that city, shake off the very dust from your feet for a testimony against them. Herod heard of all that is done by Him and he is perplexed because some says John is risen from the dead; and some, that Elias has appear; and others, one of the old prophets is risen again. Herod says, John I have beheaded: but who is this, of whom I hear such things? And he desired to see Him.

His own people rejected Jesus for they are offended by Him, having prejudices and biases against Him until He could not do many mighty works among them because of their unbelief. Herod knew John was a righteous and holy man, imprisoned him at first, but overtime, became hardened, gave in to his own covetous heart and darkened mind, and executed an innocent man and prophet.

Walking On the Sea & the Wind Ceased (6:30-56)

The messengers came to Jesus, and told Him all things, both what they did, and what they had taught. He says to them, Come apart into a desert place, and rest a while. There were many coming and going, and they had no leisure so much as to eat. They departed into a desert place by boat privately. People saw them departing, and many who knew Him ran on foot out of all cities, and outran them, and came together to Him. Jesus, when He came out, saw many people, was moved with compassion toward them, because they were as sheep without a Shepherd: and He began to teach them many things. The day was now far spent, His disciples came to Him, and say, This is a desert place, and now the time is far passed: send them away, that they may go into the country villages, and buy themselves bread: for they have nothing to eat. He answers and say to them, Give them to eat. They say to Him, Shall we go and buy twenty dollars of bread, and give them to eat? He says to them, How many loaves do you have? Go and see. When they knew, they say, Five, and two fishes. He commanded them to make all sit down by groups on the green grass. They sat down in rows of hundreds, and fifties. When He had taken the five loaves and two fishes, He looked up to heaven and blessed, broke the loaves and gave them to His disciples to set before them and the two fishes He divided among them all. They did all eat, and were filled. They took up twelve baskets full of the fragments, and of the fishes. Those who eat of the loaves were about five thousand men. Straightaway He constrained His disciples to get into the boat to go to the other side to Bethsaida, while He sent away the people. When He had sent them away, He departed to a mountain to pray. When evening comes, the boat was in the midst of the sea, and He was alone on land. He saw them toiling in rowing; for the wind was contrary to them: and about four o'clock in the morning He came to them, walking on the sea, and would have passed by them. When they saw Him walking on the sea, they supposed it had been a spirit, and cried out: they all saw Him and were troubled. Immediately He talked with them, and says to them, Be of good cheer: it is I; be not afraid. He went up to them into the boat; and the wind ceased. They were sore amazed in themselves beyond measure, and wondered. For they considered not the miracle of the loaves: for their heart was hardened. When they had passed over, they came to the land of Gennesaret, and drew to the shore. When they come out of the boat, straightaway they knew Him, and ran through that whole region and began to carry about in beds those who were sick, where they heard He was. Whichever villages, cities, or country He entered, they laid the sick in the streets, and begged Him to touch the border of His garment: and as many as touched Him were made whole.

Those men, when they saw the miracle He did, say, Truly, this is the prophet to come into the world. Jesus perceived they had come to take Him by force to make Him a king, straightaway constrained His disciples to get into a boat, while He sent the multitude away. He went up a mountain to pray alone. The boat was in the midst of the sea, tossed about with waves: for the wind was contrary. At four o'clock in the morning Jesus went to them, walking on the sea. When the disciples saw Him walking on the sea, they are troubled, saying, It is a ghost; and they cry out for fear. Straightaway Jesus speaks to them, saying, Be of good cheer; it is I; be not afraid. Peter answers Him and say, Master, if it is You, command me come to You on the water. He says, Come. Peter gets out of the boat, walk on the water to go to Jesus. But when he saw the boisterous wind, he became afraid and began to sink, he cries out, saying, Master, save me. Immediately Jesus stretch forth His hand, catches him and says to him, You of little faith, why did you doubt? When they came into the boat, the wind ceased. Those who are in the boat came and worshipped Him, saying, Truly, You are the Son of God.

Even in the desert place, a multitude flock to Jesus who has compassion on them for they are like sheep without a Shepherd. He teaches and feeds them before going to a mountain alone to pray because some men tried to make Him King, seeing He is that prophet who is to come to the world. Messiah King. Walks on water. The wind ceased. They worshipped Him, The Son of God. Jesus is more than a moral teacher, more than a prophet or earthly king.

What Comes Out of A Person Defiles the Person (7:1-23)

Then came to Him the Pharisees and certain scribes from Jerusalem. When they saw some of His disciples eat bread with defiled, that is to say, with unwashed hands, they found fault. For the Pharisees and the Jews, except they wash their hands, eat not, holding the tradition of the elders. When they come from the market, except they wash, they eat not. Many other things which they have received to hold, as the washing of cups and pots, copper vessels and tables. The Pharisees and scribes ask Him, Why walk not your disciples according to the tradition of the elders, but eat bread with unwashed hands? He answers and say to them, Well has Isaiah prophesied of you hypocrites, as it is written, This people honours Me with their lips, but their heart is far from Me. In vain do they worship Me, teaching for doctrines the commandments of men. For laying aside the commandment of God, you hold the tradition of men, as the washing of pots and cups: and many other such things you do. He says to them, Full well you reject God's commandment to keep your own tradition. Moses said, Honour your father and mother; whoever curses father or mother, let him be put to death: but you say, If a man say to his father or mother, It is Korban, that is to say, a gift, by whatever you might benefit by me; he shall be free. You permit him no more to do anything for his father or mother; making God's word ineffectual through your tradition, which you delivered and many such things you do. When He had called all the people to Him, He says to them, Hearken to Me every one of you, and understand: There is nothing from outside, entering in can defile a person: but the things which come out of him or her, those defile the person. If any one have ears to hear, let him or her hear. When He entered into the house, His disciples asked Him concerning the parable. He says to them, Are you without understanding also? Do you not perceive, that whatever thing from outside enters in cannot defile the person, because it enters not into their heart, but the belly and passes out as waste? He says, What comes out of a person defiles the person. For from within, out of the heart of people, proceed evil thoughts, adulteries, sexual immorality, murders, thefts, covetousness, wickedness, deceit, lasciviousness, an evil eye, blasphemy, pride, foolishness: All these evil things come from within and defile the person.

Then came scribes and Pharisees to Jesus from Jerusalem, saying, Why do Your disciples transgress the tradition of the elders? He answers and say to them, Why do you transgress God's commandment by your tradition? You hypocrites, well did Isaiah prophesy of you, saying, This people draw near to Me and honour Me with their lips; but their heart is far from Me. In vain they worship Me, teaching for doctrines the commandments of men.

He calls the multitude and says to them, Hear, and understand: it is not what enter the mouth that defiles a person; but what comes out of the mouth, this defile a person. His disciples say to Him, Do You know the Pharisees are offended by this saying? He answers and say, Every plant which My heavenly Father has not planted, shall be rooted up. Leave them alone: they are blind leaders leading the blind, and both shall fall into the ditch.

Peter says to Him, Declare to us this parable. Jesus says, Are you also yet without understanding? Do you still not understand that whatever enter in the mouth goes into the belly, and passes out as waste? But those things which proceed out of the mouth come forth from the heart; and they defile the person. For out of the heart proceed evil thoughts, murders, adulteries, sexual immorality, thefts, false witness, blasphemies. These are the things which defile a person but to eat with unwashed hands defile not him or her.

Out of the abundance of the heart, the mouth speaks. With it one blesses God, and curses his or her brother and sister made in God the Father's image. Can bitter and sweet water come from the same spring? Can the fig tree bear olive berries? Or a vine, figs? So neither can any spring both yield salt water and fresh. Every plant not of the heavenly Father shall be uprooted, for His plantings are oaks of righteousness: comfort those who mourn, exchange beauty for ashes; unlike leaders led by their own light fall into the ditch of covetousness, delusion and presumption with their blind followers.

He Makes the Deaf Hear; the Dumb Speak (7:24-37)

From there He arose, went to the borders of Tyre and Sidon, entered into a house, and would have no one know it: but He could not be hid. A certain woman, whose young daughter had an unclean spirit, heard of Him, and came and fell at His feet: she was a Greek, a Syrophenician by ethnicity; and begged Him to cast the devil out of her daughter. Jesus says to her, Let the children first be filled: for it is not right to take the children's bread, and to cast it to the dogs. She answers and say to Him, Yes, Master: yet the dogs under the table eat the children's crumbs. He says to her, For this saying go your way; the devil is gone out of your daughter. When she come to her house, she found the devil gone and her daughter laid upon the bed. Departing from the coasts of Tyre and Sidon, He came to the sea of Galilee, through the midst of the coasts of Decapolis. They brought to Him one deaf who had an impediment in his speech; and they beseech Him to put His hand on him. He took him aside from the multitude, put His fingers into his ears, spit and touched his tongue; looking up to heaven, He sighed, and says to him, Ephphatha, that is, Be opened. Straightaway his ears were opened, his tongue loosed, and he spoke plainly. He charged them to tell no one: but the more He charged them, the more they published it; and were beyond measure astonished, saying, He has done all things well: He makes the deaf hear, the dumb speak.

Jesus went and departed into the coasts of Tyre and Sidon. Behold, a woman of Canaan comes out of the same coasts, and cries to Him, saying, Have mercy on me, O Master, Son of David; my daughter is grievously vexed with a devil. He answered her not a word. His disciples come and beseech Him, saying, Send her away; for she cries after us. He answers and say, I am sent to the lost sheep of the house of Israel. Then she comes and worship Him, saying, Master, help me. He answers and say, It is not right to take the children's bread, and to cast it to dogs. She says, True, Master: yet the dogs eat the crumbs which fall from their master's' table. Jesus answers and say to her, O woman, great is your faith: be it unto you even as you desired. And her daughter was made whole from that very hour. Jesus departed from there, and come near to the sea of Galilee; goes up a mountain, and sits down there. And a great multitude come to Him, having with them those who are lame, blind, dumb, maimed, and many others, and cast them down at Jesus' feet; and He healed them: so much the multitude wondered when they see the dumb speak, the maimed made whole, the lame walk, the blind see: and they glorify the God of Israel.

A nameless Greek woman of Syrophoenician ethnicity, a gentile who is a non-Jew sought Jesus to heal her daughter with an unclean spirit. She recognised Jesus as Master and Son of David, the promised Messiah. When Jesus told her His ministry was to Jewish people, implying that gentiles and non-Jews are excluded, she was not daunted but pleaded that even dogs deserve the crumbs that fall from the master's table. Seeing her great faith, Jesus delivered her daughter from the devil with a word without seeing nor touching her. Throughout Israel, Jesus cast out unclean spirits, restore hearing, sight, speech, limbs made whole. The people wonder and glorify the God of Israel, praising Jesus for doing all things well: He makes the deaf hear, the dumb speak.

To be made whole is more than just physical healing and restoration of the use of the senses and faculties, but also to hear attentively the word of deliverance; to live a life of faith and allegiance to Messiah Jesus; and to testify the good news of the kingdom of God which is more than food and drink: it is righteousness, and peace and joy in the Holy Spirit. Jesus heal, restore, made us whole to be free from Satan's oppression, courage to face the world's opposition, to publish the good news of the kingdom of God is here. The good news is preach to the Jews first but also to the nations. It is the power of God for deliverance to everyone who believes. Repent and believe. For the righteousness of God is revealed from faith to faith. The righteous shall live by faith.

Is Your Heart Still Hardened? (8:1-21)

In those days the great multitude have nothing to eat. Jesus called His disciples to Him, and says to them, I have compassion on the multitude, because they have been with Me three days and have nothing to eat. If I send them away fasting to their own houses, they will faint by the way: for many of them came from far. His disciples answer Him, Can anyone satisfy these men with bread here in the wilderness? He asks them, How many loaves do you have? They said, Seven. He commanded the people to sit down on the ground. He took the seven loaves and gave thanks, broke and gave to His disciples to set before them; and they set them before the people. They had a few small fishes He blessed and commanded to set them before them. They ate and were filled: and took up the broken meat that was left seven baskets. Those eaten were about four thousand: and He sent them away. Straightaway He entered into a boat with His disciples, and came into the parts of Dalmanutha. The Pharisees came and began to question Him, seeking of Him a sign from heaven, tempting Him. He sighed deeply in His spirit, and says, Why does this generation seek after a sign? Truly I say to you, There shall no sign be given to this generation. He left them, and entering into the boat again departed to the other side. Now the disciples had forgotten to take bread, neither had they in the boat with them more than one loaf. He charged them, saying, Take heed, beware of the leaven of the Pharisees, and of the leaven of Herod. They reasoned among themselves, saying, It is because we have no bread. When Jesus knew it, He says to them, Why reason because you have no bread? Do you not perceive yet, neither understand? Is your heart still hardened? Having eyes, see not? Having ears, hear not? Do you not remember? When I broke the five loaves among five thousand, how many baskets full of fragments you took up? Twelve. When the seven among four thousand, how many baskets full of fragments you took up? Seven. He says to them, How is it that you do not understand?

Jesus calls His disciples and say, I have compassion on the multitude because they continue with Me three days and have nothing to eat. His disciples say to Him, Is there bread in the wilderness to fill so great a multitude? Jesus says to them, How many loaves do you have? Seven and a few little fishes. He commands the multitude to sit on the ground. He takes the seven loaves and fishes, give thanks, breaks them, give to His disciples, and the disciples to the multitude. They all ate and are full: they picked up the broken meat into seven full baskets. Those who ate were four thousand men, besides women and children.

The Pharisees with the Sadducees come, tempting Him to show them a sign from heaven. He answers and say to them, When it is evening, you say, It will be fair weather: for the sky is red. And in the morning, It will be foul weather today: for the sky is red and rumbling. O you hypocrites, you can discern the face of the sky; but you cannot discern the signs of the times? A wicked and adulterous generation seeks after a sign; and there shall be no sign given, but the sign of the prophet Jonas. He left them and departed. When His disciples goes to the other side, they forgot to take bread. Jesus says to them, Take heed and beware the leaven of the Pharisees and the Sadducees. They reason among themselves, saying, It is because we have taken no bread. When Jesus perceives it, He says to them, O you of little faith, why reason among yourselves, because you brought no bread? Do you not yet understand, neither remember the five loaves of the five thousand, and how many baskets you took up? Neither the seven loaves of the four thousand, and how many baskets you took up? Why do you not understand I speak not concerning bread, that you beware the leaven of the Pharisees and of the Sadducees? Then they understood He bids them not beware of the leaven of bread, but of their teachings.

The leaven of the Pharisees and Sadducees is hypocrisy, teaching to obey scriptures but not practicing themselves. The leaven of Herod is doublemindedness: serving God and mammon with greed and immorality, taking his brother's wife contrary to God's law, abusing his position by executing John, an innocent man.

Who Do You Say That I Am? (8:22-38)

He comes to Bethsaida; they brought a blind man to Him, and begged Him to touch him. He took the blind man by the hand, led him out of town; and when He had spit on his eyes, put His hands on him, He asked him if he saw anything. He looked up, and says, I see men as trees, walking. He put His hands again on his eyes and made him look up: he was restored and saw every man clearly. He sent him away to his house, saying, Neither go into town, nor tell anyone in the town. Jesus and His disciples went into the towns of Caesarea Philippi and by the way He asks His disciples, saying to them, Whom do men say I am? They answer, John the Baptist: some say, Elias; and others, One of the prophets. He says to them, But who do you say that I am? Peter answers and say to Him, You are the Messiah. He charged them to tell no one of Him. He began to teach them the Son of man must suffer many things, be rejected by the elders, chief priests and scribes, be killed, and after three days rise again. He spoke that saying openly. Peter took Him, and began to rebuke Him. When He turned around, looking on His disciples, He rebuked Peter, saying, Get you behind Me, Satan: for you savour not the things of God, but the things of men. When He called the people to Him with His disciples, He says to them, Whoever comes after Me, shall deny himself or herself, take up his or her cross, and follow Me. Anyone who save one's life shall lose it; but anyone who loses one's life for My sake and the gospel's, the same shall deliver it. What shall a person profit, if one gain the whole world and loses one's own soul? Or what shall one give in exchange for one's soul? Whoever is ashamed of Me and My words in this adulterous and sinful generation; of him or her shall the Son of Man be ashamed, when He comes in His Father's glory with the holy angels.

When Jesus came to the coasts of Caesarea Philippi, He asks His disciples, Whom do men say that I the Son of Man am? Some say You are John the Baptist: some, Elias; and others, Jeremiah, or one of the prophets. He says to them, But whom say you that I am? Simon Peter answers and say, You are the Messiah, the Son of the living God. Jesus answers and say to him, Blessed are you, Simon Bar–jona: for flesh and blood has not revealed it to you, but My

Father in heaven. I say to you, You are Peter, upon this rock I will build My church; and the gates of hell shall not prevail against it. I will give you the keys of the kingdom of heaven: whatever you bind on earth shall be bound in heaven: and whatever you loose on earth shall be loosed in heaven. Then He charge His disciples to tell no one He is Jesus the Messiah. From then on, Jesus begin to show to His disciples, how He must go to Jerusalem, and suffer many things of the elders, chief priests and scribes, be killed, and rise again the third day. Then Peter taking Him, begin to rebuke Him, saying, Be it far from You, Lord: this shall not happen to You. But He turn, and say to Peter, Get you behind Me, Satan: you are an offence to Me: for you savour not the things of God, but those of men. Then says Jesus to His disciples, Whoever comes after Me, shall deny himself or herself, take up their cross, and follow Me. Whoever will save his or her life shall lose it: and whoever will lose one's life for My sake shall find it. What does a person profit, if one gain the whole world, and loses one's own soul? What shall one give in exchange for one's soul? For the Son of Man shall come in His Father's glory with His angels; and He shall reward every one according to their works.

Many of His disciples went back, and walked no more with Him. Jesus says to the twelve, Will you also go away? Simon Peter answers Him, Master, to whom shall we go? You have the words of eternal life. We believe and are sure that You are Messiah, the Son of the living God. Jesus answers them, Have I not chosen twelve, and one of you is a devil? He speaks of Judas Iscariot the son of Simon: for he is the one who betrays Him, being one of the twelve.

Whom do others say, I the Son of Man am? Jesus asked this to know the popular opinions and impressions others have of Him. He asked His disciples, But who do you say that I am? From his daily encounter with Jesus' first hand, Peter confess, You are the Messiah, the Son of the living God. Now, who do you personally say Jesus is?

This is My Beloved Son, Hear Him (9:1-29)

He says to them, Truly I say to you, There be some standing here, who shall not taste death, till they have seen the kingdom of God come with power. After six days Jesus takes Peter, James, and John, and lead them up into an high mountain apart by themselves: and He was transfigured before them. His raiment became shining, exceeding white as snow; so as no launderer on earth can white them. There appeared to them Elias with Moses: and they were talking with Jesus. Peter answers and say to Jesus, Master, it is good for us to be here: let us make three tents; one for You, one for Moses, and one for Elias. He did not know what else to say; for they were sore afraid. There was a cloud overshadowing them: and a Voice came out of the cloud, saying, This is My beloved Son: hear Him. Suddenly, when they looked round about, they saw no man any more, except Jesus only with themselves. As they came down from the mountain, He charged them to tell no one what they had seen, till the Son of Man is risen from the dead. They kept that saying with themselves, questioning one with another what the rising from the dead mean. They ask Him, saying, Why do the scribes say Elias must first come? He answers and tell them, Elias truly comes first, and restore all things; and how it is written of the Son of Man, that He must suffer many things, despised and contempt. But I say to you, That Elias is indeed come, and they have done to him whatever they listed, as it is written of him. When He came to His disciples, He saw a great multitude about them, and the scribes questioning them. Straightaway all the people, when they beheld Him, were greatly amazed, and running to Him, saluted Him. He asks the scribes, What question do you have with them? One of the multitude answers and say, Master, I brought You my son, who has a dumb spirit; and wherever he takes him, he tears him: foams, gnashes his teeth and pines away: and I spoke to Your disciples they should cast him out; and they could not. He answers him, and says, O faithless generation, how long shall I be with you? How long shall I bear with you? Bring him to Me. They brought him to Him. When he saw Him, straightaway the spirit tore him; and he fell on the ground, and wallowed foaming. He asks his father, How long is it since this came to him? He says, Since a child. And often it cast him into the fire and the waters, to destroy him: but if You can do any thing, have compassion on us, and help us. Jesus says to him, If you can believe, all things are possible to him who believes. Straightaway the father of the child cries out, and say with tears, Master, I believe; help mine unbelief. When Jesus saw that the people came running together, He rebuked the foul spirit, saying to him, You dumb and deaf spirit, I charge you, come out of him, and enter no more into him. And the spirit cried, and rent him sore, and came out of him: and he was as one dead; until many said, He is dead. But Jesus took him by the hand, lifted him up; and he arose. When He comes into the house, His disciples ask Him privately, Why could we not cast him out? He says to them, This kind can come forth by nothing, but by prayer and fasting.

He takes Peter, John and James up a mountain to pray. As He prays, His countenance start to change, His clothes turn white and glistening. There talk with Him two men, Moses and Elias. Peter and those with him were heavy with sleep and when they awoke, they saw His glory, and the two men with Him. As they begin to leave Him, Peter says to Jesus, Master, it is good for us to be here. Let us make three tents; one for You, Moses, and Elias: not realising what he was saying. There comes a cloud and overshadowed them: they became afraid as they entered into the cloud. There comes a Voice out of the cloud, saying, This is My beloved Son: hear Him. When the Voice is past, Jesus is found alone. They told no one in those days any of those things which they saw. The next day, coming down from the hill, many people met Him. Behold, a man cries out, saying, Master, I implore You, look on my son: mine only child. Lo, a spirit takes him, and he cries out and it tears him that he foams again, bruising him, scarcely depart from him. I begged Your disciples to cast him out; and they could not. Jesus answers, O faithless and perverse generation, how long shall I be with you, and bear with you? Bring your son here. As he comes, the devil throws him down, and tore him. Jesus rebuke the unclean spirit, and heal the child, and deliver him again to his father. They are all amazed at God's mighty power. Jesus is God's beloved Son. Hear Him.

Every One Shall Be Salted With Fire (9:30-50)

They departed and passed through Galilee; and He would not that any one should know it. For He taught His disciples, The Son of Man is delivered into the hands of men, they shall kill Him; and after He is killed, He shall rise the third day. But they understood not that saying, and were afraid to ask Him. He came to Capernaum: and being in the house He asks them, What was it that you disputed among yourselves by the way? But they held their peace: for by the way they had disputed among themselves, who should be the greatest. He sat down and called the twelve, and says to them, If any one desire to be first, the same shall be last of all, and servant of all. He took a child, and set him in the midst of them: and when He had taken him in His arms, He says to them, Whoever shall receive one of such children in My Name, receives Me: and whoever shall receive Me, receives not Me, but Him who sent Me. John answer Him, saying, Master, we saw one casting out devils in Your Name, and he follows not us: and we forbade him, because he follows not us. Jesus says, Forbid him not: there is no one who does a miracle in My Name, can lightly speak evil of Me. For he that is not against us is with us. Whoever give you a cup of water to drink in My Name, because you belong to Messiah, truly I say to you, he shall not lose his reward. Whoever offend one of these little ones who believe in Me, it is better for him that a millstone is hung about his neck, and he is cast into the sea. If your hand offend you, cut it off: it is better for you to enter into life maimed, than having two hands cast into hellfire that never shall be quenched, where their worm dies not and the fire is not quenched. If your foot offend you, cut it off: it is better for you to enter limp into life, than having two feet cast into hellfire that never shall be quenched, where their worm dies not, and the fire is not quenched. If your eye offend you, pluck it out: it is better for you to enter into the kingdom of God with one eye, than having two eyes cast into hellfire, where their worm dies not, and the fire is not quenched. Every one shall be salted with fire, and every sacrifice shall be salted with salt. Salt is good: but if the salt loses his saltiness, how will you season it? Have salt in yourselves, and have peace one with another.

While they lodge in Galilee, Jesus says to them, The Son of Man shall be betrayed into the hands of men: They shall kill Him, and the third day He shall rise again. They are intensely sad. Let these sayings sink down into your ears: for the Son of Man shall be delivered into the hands of men. But they understand not this saying, and it is hid from them, that they perceive not: and they fear to ask Him of that saying. There arose a dispute among them, on which of them should be greatest. Jesus, perceiving the thought of their heart, took a child, and set him by Him, And says to them, Whoever shall receive this child in My Name receives Me: and whoever shall receive Me receives Him who sends Me: he who is least among you all, the same shall be great. John answers and say, Master, we saw one casting out devils in Your Name; and we forbid him, because he follows not with us. Jesus says to him, Forbid him not: for he that is not against us is for us.

Truly I say to you, Except you be converted and become as little children, you shall not enter into the kingdom of heaven. Whoever humbles himself or herself as this little child, the same is greatest in the kingdom of heaven. Anyone who receive one such little child in My Name receives Me. Anyone who offends one of these little ones which believe in Me, it is better for him or her that a millstone hung on their neck, and drown in the depth of the sea. Woe to the world because of offences! For it is necessary that offences come; but woe to that person by whom the offence comes!

All must be prepared to undergo this fiery salting in life, and they are reminded that such purgation was better by far than to be cast into hell where the fire is not quench, the sting never subsides. Salt is good; such difficulty profits a soul if they have their intended effect, that is, purge, preserve, and season the soul. But if the salt loses its saltiness—that is, if the trial does not accomplish its purging, preserving, and maturing purposes— how can anything be done for the soul or the salt? (J. Elliot)

Let the Children Come to Me (10:1-27)

He comes into the coasts of Judaea by the far side of Jordan. People flocked to Him the same as He was used to teaching them. The Pharisees came, tempting Him, ask, Is it lawful for a man to put away his wife? He answers them, What did Moses command you? They say, Moses permitted to write a bill of divorce and to put her away. Jesus answers them, For the hardness of your heart he wrote this precept. From the beginning of creation God made them male and female. For this cause a man leave his father and mother, and cleave to his wife; and the two shall be one flesh: they are no more two but one flesh. What God joined together, let no one pull apart. In the house, His disciples ask Him again on the same matter. He says to them, Whoever put away his wife and marry another, commits adultery against her. If a woman put away her husband and marry another, she commits adultery. They brought young children for Him to touch them and His disciples rebuked those who brought them. When Jesus saw it, He was much displeased and says to them, Let the children come to Me and forbid not: for such is the kingdom of God. Truly I say to you, Whoever does not receive God's kingdom as a little child, shall not enter in. He took them up in His arms, put His hands on them and blessed them. When He went forth into the way, there came one running, kneeled and ask Him, Good Master, what shall I do to inherit eternal life? Jesus says to him, Why call Me good? There is none good but God. You know the commandments, Do not commit adultery, Do not kill, Do not steal, Do not bear false witness, Defraud not, Honour your father and mother. He answers and say to Him, Master, all these have I observed from my youth. Jesus beholding him, loved him, and says, One thing you lack: go your way, sell what you have, give to the poor and you shall have treasure in heaven: come, take up the cross, and follow Me. He was sad at that saying and went away grieved: for he had great possessions. Jesus looked around and says to His disciples, How hard shall those who have riches enter into God's kingdom! The disciples were astonished at His words. Jesus answers again and say to them, Children, how hard is it for those who trust in riches to enter into God's kingdom! It is easier for a camel to pass through a needle's eye, than for a rich man to enter God's kingdom. They were astonished beyond measure, saying among themselves, Who then can be delivered? Jesus, looking on them says, With men it is impossible, but not with God: for with God all things are possible.

Is it lawful for a man to put away his wife for any cause? He answers and say to them, Have you not read, He who made them at the beginning made them male and female, and say, For this cause shall a man leave father and mother, cleave to his wife and the two shall be one flesh? Therefore they are no more two but one flesh. What therefore God has join together, let no one separate. This is a great mystery: but I speak of Messiah and the church. Let every one loves his wife as himself; and the wife respects her husband.

Anyone who put away their spouse, except for sexual immorality, and marry another, commits adultery, and whoever marries the latter commit adultery. His disciples say to Him, If the case for both are the same, it is not good to marry. He says to them, All cannot receive this saying, except those to whom it is given. There are some singles, who were born from their mother's womb; there are some singles, who were made single by people; and there are singles, who have made themselves singles for the kingdom of heaven's sake. Anyone who is able to receive it, let them receive it.

Then were brought to Him little children, that He should put His hands on them, and pray: and the disciples rebuked them. But Jesus says, Let the little children, and forbid them not, to come to Me: for of such is the kingdom of heaven.

Then says Jesus to His disciples, Truly I say to you, A rich person shall hardly enter into the kingdom of heaven. And again I say to you, It is easier for a camel to go through the eye of a needle, than for a rich person to enter the kingdom of God. When His disciples heard it, they are exceedingly amazed, saying, Who then can be delivered? Jesus, beholding them, says, With men this is impossible; but with God all things are possible.

Many Who Are First Shall Be Last (10:28-45)

Peter began to say to Him, Lo, we have left all, and have followed
You. Jesus answers and say, Truly I say to you, The one who left
house, brothers, sisters, father, mother, wife, children, or lands, for
My sake and the gospel's, shall receive an hundredfold now in this
time, houses, brothers, sisters, mothers, children, lands, with
persecutions; and in the age to come eternal life. Many who are first
shall be last; and the last first. They were in the way going up to
Jerusalem; and Jesus went before them. They were amazed; and as
they followed, they were afraid. He took again the twelve, and
began to tell them what things should happen to Him, saying,
Behold, we go up to Jerusalem; and the Son of Man shall be
delivered to the chief priests and the scribes; they shall condemn
Him to death and deliver Him to the nations. They shall mock Him
and scourge Him, spit on Him and kill Him: and the third day He
shall rise again. James and John, the sons of Zebedee, come to Him,
saying, Master, we would that You should do for us whatever we
shall desire. He says to them, What would you that I should do for
you? They say to Him, Grant to us that we may sit, one on Your right
hand, and the other on Your left hand, in Your glory. Jesus says to
them, You know not what you ask: can you drink of the cup that I
drink of? Be baptised with the baptism that I am baptised with?
They say to Him, We can. Jesus says to them, You shall indeed drink
of the cup that I drink of and be baptised with the baptism that I
am baptised with. But to sit on My right hand and on My left hand
is not Mine to give; but it shall be given to them for whom it is
prepared. When the ten heard it, they began to be much displeased
with James and John. Jesus called and says to them, You know that
those who rule over the nations are tyrants and their leaders
become dictators. But it shall not be so among you: the one who
want to be great shall be your servant, and the one who want to be
first shall be slave of all. For even the Son of man came not to be
served, but to serve, and to give His life a ransom for many.

Peter says to Him, Behold, we have forsaken all, and followed
You; what shall we have therefore? Jesus says to them, Truly I say to
you, you who follow Me, in the regeneration when the Son of Man
shall sit on the throne of His glory, you shall sit on twelve thrones,

judging the twelve tribes of Israel. Every one who forsake houses, brothers, sisters, father, mother, wife, children, or lands, for My Name's sake, shall receive an hundredfold, and inherit everlasting life. But many who are first shall be last; and the last shall be first.

Jesus goes up to Jerusalem, takes the twelve disciples aside on the way and says to them, Behold, we go up to Jerusalem and the Son of Man shall be betrayed to the chief priests and the scribes, they shall condemn Him to death, deliver Him to the nations to mock, scourge, and crucify Him: the third day He shall rise again. Then comes to Him the mother of Zebedee's children with her sons, worshipping Him, and desiring a certain thing from Him. He says to her, What do you want? She says to Him, Grant my two sons to sit, one on Your right hand and the other on the left, in Your kingdom. Jesus answers and say, You know not what you ask. Are you able to drink the cup I shall drink, and to be baptise with the baptism that I am baptised with? They say to Him, We are able. He says to them, You shall drink indeed of My cup, and be baptise with the baptism that I am baptised with: but to sit on My right hand, and on My left, is not Mine to give, but it shall be given for whom it is prepared by My Father. When the ten heard it, they are moved with indignation against the two brothers. But Jesus calls them to Him, and says, You know the princes of the nations exercise dominion over them, and they who are great exercise authority upon them. But it shall not be so among you: whoever will be great among you, shall be your servant; and whoever will be chief among you, shall be your slave: Even as the Son of Man came not to be served, but to serve, and to give His life a ransom for many.

The path to greatness is servanthood. A leader serves and is a slave of all. The Jews expected their Messiah King to be a great and mighty warrior who will deliver them from Roman servitude but Jesus says He came to serve and give His life a ransom for many.

Jesus, Son of David (10:46-11:14)

They came to Jericho: and as He went out of Jericho with His disciples and a great number of people, blind Bartimaeus, the son of Timaeus, sat by the highway side begging. When he heard that it was Jesus of Nazareth, he began to cry out, Jesus, Son of David, have mercy on me. Many charged him to hold his peace: but he cried all the more, Son of David, have mercy on me. Jesus stood still, and commanded him to be called. They call the blind man, saying to him, Be of good comfort, rise; He calls you. And he, casting away his garment, rose, and came to Jesus. Jesus answers and say to him, What will you that I do to you? The blind man says to Him, Master, that I might receive my sight. Jesus says to him, Go your way; your faith has made you whole. Immediately he received his sight, and followed Jesus in the way. When they came near Jerusalem, to Bethphage and Bethany, at the mount of Olives, He sends forth two of His disciples, and say to them, Go your way into the village on the other side and as soon as you enter it, you shall find a colt tied, on which no one has sat before; loose him, and bring him. And if any one say to you, Why do you this? say you that the Master needs him; and straightaway he will send him here. They went their way, and found the colt tied by the door in a place where two ways meet; and they loose him. And certain of them that stood there say to them, Why are you untying the colt? And they say to them even as Jesus had commanded: and they let them go. They brought the colt to Jesus, and cast their garments on him; and He sat upon him. Many spread their garments in the way: and others cut down branches off the trees, and strewn them in the way. They that went before, and they that followed, cried, saying, Hosanna; Blessed is He who comes in the Name of the Lord: Blessed be the kingdom of our father David, that comes in the Name of the Lord: Hosanna in the highest. Jesus entered into Jerusalem, and into the temple: and when He had looked round about upon all things, and now the evening comes, He went out to Bethany with the twelve. The next day, when they come from Bethany, He was hungry. Seeing a fig tree afar off having leaves, He came, if perhaps He might find any thing on it, and when He came to it, He found nothing but leaves; for the time of figs was not yet. Jesus answers and say to it, No one eat fruit of you hereafter forever. And His disciples heard it.

As He came near to Jericho, a certain blind man sits by the wayside begging: And hearing the multitude pass by, he asks what it means. And they tell him, that Jesus of Nazareth passes by. He cries, saying, Jesus, Son of David, have mercy on me. Those who went before rebuke him, that he should hold his peace: but he cries so much the more, Son of David, have mercy on me. Jesus stood still and commanded him to be brought to Him: and when he comes near, He asks him, saying, What will you that I do to you? And he says, Master, that I may receive my sight. Jesus says to him, Receive your sight: your faith has delivered you. Immediately he receives his sight, and follows Him, glorifying God: and all the people, when they saw it, praise God. A blind man recognises Jesus, Son of David.

When they came near to Jerusalem, to Bethphage, and Mount Olives, Jesus sends two disciples, saying to them, Go into the village over against you, and straightaway you shall find an ass tied, and a colt with her: loose them, and bring them to Me. And if any one ask why are you doing this, say, The Master has need of them; and straightaway he will send them. All this is done to fulfill what was spoken by the prophet, saying, Tell the daughter of Zion, Behold, your King comes to you, righteous and victorious, meek and riding upon an ass, and a colt, the foal of an ass.

Those, who like blind Bartimaeus, recognises Jesus as the Son of David fulfilling Zechariah's prophecy of Israel's coming King, humble and meek, riding on an ass and her colt into Jerusalem with the crowd waving palm leaves and spreading branches on the way into the holy city, shouting: Blessed is He who comes in the Name of the Lord. Blessed be the kingdom of our father David, that comes in the Name of the Lord. Hosanna in the highest. Jesus' triumphal entry into Jerusalem riding on an ass is hardly what many Jews would expect of a coming Messiah King to liberate them from Roman rule. Yet in fulfilment of prophecy was never in doubt.

House of Prayer for All Nations (11:15-33)

They come to Jerusalem: and Jesus went into the temple, and began to cast out those who sold and bought in the temple, overthrew the tables of the moneychangers and the seats of those who sold doves; and permitted no one to carry any vessel through the temple. He taught, saying to them, Is it not written, My house shall be called the house of prayer for all nations? You have made it a den of thieves. The scribes and chief priests heard it, and sought how they might destroy Him: for they feared Him, because all the people was astonished at His teaching. When evening comes, He went out of the city. In the morning, as they passed by, they saw the fig tree dried up from the roots. Peter calling to remembrance says to Him, Master, behold, the fig tree which You cursed is withered away. Jesus answering says to them, Have faith in God. For truly I say to you, Whoever shall say to this mountain, be removed and cast into the sea and not doubt in their heart, but believe those things which one says shall come to pass; one shall have whatever one says. I say to you, Whatever things you desire, when you pray, believe that you receive them and you shall have them. When you stand praying, forgive, if you have anything against anyone, that your Father in heaven may forgive your trespasses. But if you do not forgive, neither will your Father in heaven forgive your trespasses. They come again to Jerusalem. As He was walking in the temple, there come to Him the chief priests, the scribes and the elders, and say to Him, By what authority You do these things? Who gave You this authority to do these things? Jesus answers, I will also ask you one question, and answer Me, I will tell you by what authority I do these things. The baptism of John was from heaven or men? Answer Me. They reason among themselves, saying, If we say, From heaven; He will say, Why then did you not believe him? If we say, Of men; they feared the people, for all men counted John a prophet indeed. They answer and say to Jesus, We cannot tell. Jesus answering says to them, neither do I tell you by what authority I do these things.

When He came to Jerusalem, all the city stirred, saying, Who is this? The multitude says, This is Jesus the prophet of Nazareth of Galilee. Jesus goes into the temple of God, and cast out all who sells and buys in the temple, overthrow the tables of the moneychangers, the seats of those who sell doves, and says to them, It is written, My house shall be called the house of prayer; but you have made it a den of thieves. The blind and the lame come to Him in the temple; and He heals them. When the chief priests and scribes saw the wonderful things He did and the children crying in the temple, and saying, Hosanna to the Son of David; they are sore displease, and say to Him, Do You hear what they say? Jesus says to them, Yes; have you never read, Out of the mouth of babes and sucklings You have perfect praise? And He teaches daily in the temple. But the chief priests, scribes and the chief of the people seek to destroy Him, and finds nothing to do so: for all the people are very attentive to hear Him. He leaves them and goes out of the city into Bethany.

When He saw a fig tree on the way, He found nothing but leaves only, and says to it, Let no fruit grow on you henceforth for ever. Presently the fig tree withers away. When the disciples saw it, they marvel, saying, How quickly the fig tree withers away! Jesus says to them, Truly I say to you, If you have faith and doubt not, you shall not only do this to the fig tree, but say to this mountain, Be remove, and be cast into the sea; it shall be done. And all things, whatever you asks in prayer, believing, you shall receive. When He comes to the temple, the chief priests and elders come as He is teaching, and say, By what authority do You these things? Who give You this authority? Jesus says to them, I also will ask you one thing, which if you tell Me, I will tell you by what authority I do these things. The baptism of John, where did it come from? From heaven, or of men? They reason with themselves, saying, If we say, From heaven; He will say to us, Why did you not then believe him? But if we say, Of men; we fear the people; for all hold John as a prophet. They answer Jesus, We cannot tell. He says to them, Neither do I tell you by what authority I do these things. Have faith in God. God answers the prayers of those who forgive others who sinned against them.

The Stone Rejected is the Chief Cornerstone (12:1-17)

He began to speak to them by parables. A certain man planted a vineyard, set an hedge about it, digged a place for the winefat, built a tower, let it out to vine growers and went into a far country. At the season he sent to the vine growers a servant, that he might receive from the vine growers of the fruit of the vineyard. They caught him, beat him, and sent him away empty. He sent to them another servant; at him they cast stones, wounded him in the head and sent him away shamefully handled. He sent another and him they killed, and many others; beating some and killing some. Having yet therefore one son, his wellbeloved, he sent him also last to them, saying, They will reverence my son. But those vine growers said among themselves, This is the heir; come, let us kill him, and the inheritance shall be ours. They took him, killed him and cast him out of the vineyard. What shall therefore the master of the vineyard do? He will come and destroy the vine growers, and will give the vineyard to others. Have you not read this scripture; The stone which the builders rejected is become the head of the corner: This was the Lord's doing, and it is marvellous in our eyes? They sought to lay hold on Him, but feared the people: for they knew He had spoken the parable against them: they left Him and went their way. They send to Him certain Pharisees and the Herodians, to catch Him in His words. When they come, they say to Him, Master, we know that You are true, and care for no one: for You regard not the person of men, but teaches the way of God in truth: Is it lawful to give tribute to Caesar, or not? Shall we give, or shall we not give? But He, knowing their hypocrisy, said to them, Why tempt you Me? Bring me a coin, that I may see it. They brought it. He says to them, Whose image and superscription is this? They said to Him, Caesar's. Jesus answering said to them, Render to Caesar the things of Caesar's, and to God the things of God's. They marvelled at Him.

When the time of the harvest draws near, the master of the vineyard sends his servants to the vine growers, that they receive the fruits of it. The vine growers take his servants, beat one, kill another, and stone the other. He sends other servants more than the first: and they did to them the same. Last of all he sends his son, saying, They will reverence my son. When the vine growers sees the son, they say among themselves, This is the heir; come, let us kill him, and seize his inheritance. They caught him, cast him out of the vineyard, and slew him. When the master of the vineyard comes, what will he do to those vine growers? They say to Him, he will miserably destroy those wicked men, and let out his vineyard to other vine growers, who shall render him the fruits in their seasons. Jesus says to them, Did you not read in the scriptures, The stone which the builders rejected, the same is become the head of the corner: this is the Lord's doing, and it is marvellous in our eyes? I say to you, God's kingdom shall be taken from you, and given to a nation bringing forth the fruits thereof. Anyone who falls on this stone shall be broken: but on whomever it falls, it will crush them.

The priests, the captain of the temple, and the Sadducees, come upon them, grieved they taught the people, and preached through Jesus, the resurrection from the dead. Many heard the word, believed; the number of the men was about five thousand. The next day, their rulers, elders, scribes, Annas the high priest, Caiaphas, John, and Alexander, and as many as are the kindred of the high priest, gather together at Jerusalem. They ask, By what power, or by what name, have you done this? Peter, filled with the Holy Spirit, says to them, You rulers of the people, and elders of Israel, If we this day be examined of the good deed done to the impotent man, by what means he is made whole; Be it known to you, and the people of Israel, by the Name of Messiah Jesus of Nazareth, whom you crucified, whom God raised from the dead, by Him does this man stand here before you whole. This is the stone which was rejected by you builders, which is become the head of the corner. There is deliverance in no other: there is no other Name under heaven given among mankind, whereby we must be delivered. They saw the boldness of Peter and John, perceived they were unlearned and ignorant men; marvelled and realised they had been with Jesus.

More Than Offerings & Sacrifices (12:18-44)

Then come to Him the Sadducees who say there is no resurrection. They ask Him, saying, Master, Moses wrote to us, If a man's brother die, leave his wife behind him and no children, that his brother should take his wife and raise up seed to his brother. Now there were seven brothers: the first took a wife and dying left no seed. The second took her and died, leaving no seed and the third likewise. The seven had her and left no seed: last of all the woman died also. In the resurrection, when they shall rise, whose wife shall she be of them? For the seven had her to wife. Jesus answering says to them, Do you not err, because you know not the scriptures, neither the power of God? When they rise from the dead, they neither marry nor are given in marriage; but are as the angels in heaven. As touching the dead, that they rise: have you not read in the book of Moses, how in the bush God spoke to him, saying, I am the God of Abraham, the God of Isaac, and the God of Jacob? He is not the God of the dead, but the God of the living: you do greatly err. One of the scribes came, having heard them reasoning together, and perceiving that He had answered them well, ask Him, Which is the first commandment of all? Jesus answers him, The first of all the commandments is, Hear, O Israel; The Lord our God is one Lord: you shall love the Lord your God with all your heart, and with all your soul, and with all your mind, and with all your strength: this is the first commandment. The second is like this, You shall love your neighbour as yourself. There is no commandment greater than these. The scribe says to Him, Well, Master, You have said the truth: for there is one God and there is none other but He: and to love Him with all the heart, and with all the understanding, and with all the soul, and with all the strength, and to love his neighbour as himself, is more than all whole burnt offerings and sacrifices. When Jesus saw that he answered discreetly, He says to him, You are not far from the kingdom of God. No one after that dare ask Him any question. Jesus answers and say, as He taught in the temple, How say the scribes that Messiah is the Son of David? For David himself said by the Holy Spirit, The Lord said to my Lord, Sit on My right hand, till I make Your enemies Your footstool. David himself calls Him Lord; how is He then his son? The common people heard Him gladly. He says to them in His teaching, Beware of the scribes who love to go in long clothing and love salutations in the marketplaces, the chief seats in the synagogues and the uppermost rooms at feasts: who devour widows' houses and for a pretence make long prayers: these shall receive greater damnation. Jesus sat over against the treasury, and beheld how the people cast money into the treasury: and many who were rich cast in much. There came a certain poor widow, and she threw in two coins, which make a penny. He called His disciples, and say to them, Truly I say to you, This poor widow cast more in, than all those who cast into the treasury: For they all cast in out of their abundance; but she out of her lack cast in all she had, even all her living.

Jesus answers and say to them, You do err, not knowing scriptures nor God's power. In the resurrection they neither marry, nor given in marriage, but are as God's angels in heaven. As touching the resurrection of the dead, have you not read what God says, I am the God of Abraham, and the God of Isaac, and the God of Jacob? God is not God of the dead, but of the living. When the multitude heard this, they are astonished at His teaching.

Master, what is the great commandment in the law? Jesus says to him, You shall love the Lord your God with all your heart, and with all your soul, and with all your mind. This is the first and great commandment. The second is like it, You shall love your neighbour as yourself. On these two commandments hang all the law and the prophets. This is God's kingdom rule and reign in Messiah Jesus.

Love works no ill to his neighbour: therefore love is the fulfilling of the law. Knowing the time, now it is high time to awake out of sleep: for now is our deliverance nearer than when we believed. The night is far spent, the day is at hand: let us cast off the works of darkness, and put on the armour of light. Let us walk honestly, as in the day; not in rioting and drunkenness, not in immorality and wantonness, not in strife and envying. Put on the Master Messiah Jesus, and make no provision for the flesh to fulfil its lusts. You are not far from the kingdom of God if you know this.

Take Heed, Watch & Pray (13:1-37)[1]

As He went out of the temple, one of His disciples say, Master, see what manner of stones and what buildings are here! Jesus answering said to him, See these great buildings? There shall not be left one stone upon another, that shall not be thrown down. As He sat on mount of Olives over against the temple, Peter, James, John and Andrew ask Him privately, Tell us, when shall these things be? What shall be the sign when all these things shall be fulfilled? Jesus answering them began to say, Take heed lest any one deceive you: many shall come in My Name, saying, I am messiah; and shall deceive many. When you hear of wars and rumours of wars, be not troubled: for such things must needs be; but the end is not yet. For nation shall rise against nation, and kingdom against kingdom: there shall be earthquakes in diverse places, famines and troubles: these are the beginnings of sorrows. Take heed to yourselves: for they shall deliver you up to councils and in the synagogues you shall be beaten: brought before rulers and kings for My sake, for a testimony against them. And the gospel must first be published among all nations. When they shall lead you and deliver you up, take no thought beforehand what you shall speak, neither do you premeditate: but whatever shall be given you in that hour, that speak: for it is not you who speak, but the Holy Spirit. Brother shall betray brother to death, father the son; children rise up against parents, and cause them to be put to death. You shall be hated by all for My Name's sake: but the one who endure to the end shall be delivered. When you see the abomination of desolation, spoken of by Daniel the prophet, standing where it ought not, (let the reader

---

[1] Mark 13, with Matthew 24 & Luke 21 are accounts of the Olivet Discourse on near future events (destruction of Jerusalem temple & end of Jewish war in 70 AD) as well as far future events: Jesus' second coming at the end of age or consummation of the age. The end will come when the gospel of the kingdom is preached and witness to all nations as Jesus' followers watch out for natural and man made disasters, famines and pestilence, wars and violence, false prophets & messiahs, persecutions and oppositions; pray for grace and mercy to endure and persevere to the end, knowing that in the last days: lawlessness will increase, love will grow cold and many people shall be deceived.

understand,) let those in Judaea flee to the mountains: let the one on the housetop not go down into the house, neither enter in, to take any thing out of the house: let one in the field not turn back again to take up his or her garment. Woe to them who are with child, and to them who give suck in those days! Pray that your flight be not in the winter. In those days shall be affliction, such as was not from the beginning of the creation which God created to this time, neither shall be. Unless the Lord had shortened those days, no flesh shall be delivered: but for the elect's sake, whom He has chosen, He has shortened the days. If any one say to you, Lo, here is messiah; or, lo, he is there; believe them not: For false messiahs and false prophets shall rise, and show signs and wonders, to seduce, if it were possible, even the elect. Take heed: behold, I have foretold you all things. In those days, after that tribulation, the sun shall be darkened, the moon shall not give her light, and the stars of heaven shall fall, and the powers that are in heaven shall be shaken. Then shall they see the Son of Man coming in the clouds with great power and glory. Then shall He send his angels, and gather together His elect from the four winds, from the uttermost part of the earth to the uttermost part of heaven. Now learn a parable of the fig tree; when her branch is yet tender, and puts forth leaves, you know that summer is near: In like manner, when you see these things come to pass, know that it is near, even at the doors. Truly I say to you, that this generation shall not pass, till all these things be done. Heaven and earth shall pass away: but My words shall not pass away. But of that day and hour knows no one, no, not the angels in heaven, neither the Son, but the Father. Take heed, watch and pray: for you know not when the time is. For the Son of Man is as a man taking a far journey, who left his house, gave authority to his servants, to every man his work and commanded the porter to watch. Watch therefore: for you know not when the master of the house comes, at evening, midnight, cockcrowing, or morning: Lest coming suddenly He finds you sleeping. And what I say to you I say to all, Watch.

As some of them spoke of the temple, how it is adorned with goodly stones and gifts, He says, As for these things which you behold, the days will come, when not one stone will be left that shall not be thrown down. And they ask Him, saying, Master, when shall these things be? What sign will there be when these things shall come to pass? And what shall be the sign of Your coming, and of the consummation of the age (συντελειας του αιωνος)?

Know you not that you are the temple of God, and the Spirit of God dwells in you? If any one defiles the temple of God, them shall God destroy; for the temple of God is holy, whose temple you are.

Be not deceived: many shall come in My Name, saying, I am messiah; the time is near, go not after them. Be not terrified. In these last days, there shall be wars and commotions, conflict and unrest, chaos and disorder, alongside pestilence and natural disasters. These are beginnings of sorrows. You will appear before authorities and rulers as a testimony against them. Settle it therefore in your hearts, not to meditate before what you shall answer. For I will give you a mouth and wisdom, which all your adversaries shall not be able to refute nor resist.

Many shall be offended, betray one another, hate one another. But there shall not an hair of your head perish. Many false prophets shall rise, and many shall be deceived. And because lawlessness shall increase, the love of many shall grow cold.

When you see the holy city surrounded with armies, know that desolation is near. Flee to the mountains. Let those who are in the midst of it run out. Let not those who are in the vicinities enter in. For these are the days of vengeance, that all things which are written may be fulfilled. But the one who endures to the end shall be delivered. In your patience, possess your souls. This gospel of the kingdom shall be preached in all the world for a witness to all nations; and then the end shall come.

But woe to those who are with child, and to those who give suck, in those days! For there shall be great distress in the land, and wrath upon this people. They shall fall by the edge of the sword, and shall be led away captive into all nations: and Jerusalem shall be trodden down by the nations, until the times of the nations be fulfilled. Blindness in part happens to Israel, until the fulness of the nations come in. And so all Israel shall be delivered: as it is written, There shall come out of Zion, the Deliverer, and shall turn away ungodliness from Jacob: for this is My covenant to them, when I shall take away their sins. As concerning the gospel, they are enemies for your sakes: but as touching the election, they are beloved for the fathers' sakes. For as you in times past have not believed God, yet have now obtain mercy through their unbelief: even so have these also now not believe, that through your mercy they also may obtain mercy. For God has concluded them all in unbelief, that He might have mercy upon everyone.

There shall be signs in the sun, moon, and stars; and on earth distress of nations with confusion; the sea and waves roar. Men's hearts fail them for fear of looking after those things which are coming on the earth; for the powers of heaven shall be shaken. As the lightning comes from the east and shines to the west, so they see the Son of Man comes in the clouds with great power and glory.

Take heed to yourselves, lest at any time your hearts are weigh down with overindulgence and drunkenness, and cares of this life, so that day catches you unawares. Like a snare, it comes on all who dwell on the face of the whole earth. Watch therefore, and pray always, that you may be accounted worthy to escape all these things that shall come to pass, and to stand before the Son of Man.

In these last days, commotions, conflicts, and pestilences are beginnings of sorrows. Persecution, betrayal, deception and violence will abound as lawlessness increases and love grows cold. Settle in your heart not to prepare in advance and let the Holy Spirit speak through you before authorities and rulers. When the holy city is surrounded by armies, the end is near but not yet, until the gospel is preached in all the world; then the end shall come. Watch.

Not My Will But Yours Be Done (14:1-36)

After two days was the feast of the passover, and of unleavened bread. The chief priests and the scribes sought how they might take Him by craft and put Him to death. But they said, Not on the feast day, lest there be an uproar of the people. Being in Bethany in the house of Simon the leper, as He sat at meat, there came a woman having an alabaster box of very precious spikenard; she broke the box and poured it on His head. There were some that had indignation within themselves, and said, Why was this waste of the ointment made? It might have been sold for a year's wage, and given to the poor. They murmured against her. Jesus says, Let her alone; why trouble her? She has wrought a good work on Me. For you have the poor with you always, and whenever you will you may do them good: but you have not Me always. She has done what she could: she anticipated and anointed My body for burial. Truly I say to you, Wherever this gospel is preached throughout the whole world, what she has done shall be spoken of for a memorial of her. Judas Iscariot, one of the twelve, went to the chief priests, to betray Him to them. When they heard it, they were glad, and promised to give him money. He sought how he might conveniently betray Him. The first day of unleavened bread, when they killed the passover, His disciples say to Him, Where do You want us to go and prepare for You to eat the passover? He sends forth two of His disciples, and says to them, Go into the city, and you shall meet a man bearing a pitcher of water: follow him. Wherever he shall go in, say to the goodman of the house, The Master says, Where is the guestchamber, where I shall eat the passover with My disciples? He will show you a large upper room furnished and prepared: there make ready for us. His disciples went forth, came into the city, and found as He had said to them: and they made ready the passover. In the evening He comes with the twelve. As they sat and eat, Jesus says, Truly I say to you, One of you who eats with Me shall betray Me. They began to be sorrowful and to say to Him one by one, Is it I? Another said, Is it I? He answers and say to them, It is one of the twelve, that dips with Me in the dish. The Son of Man indeed goes, as it is written of Him: but woe to that man by whom the Son of Man is betrayed! Good for him if he had never been born. As they eat, Jesus took bread and blessed, broke it and gave to them, and says, Take, eat: this is My body. He took the cup, and when He had given thanks, He gave it to them: and they all drank of it. He says to them, This is My blood of the new covenant, shed for many. Truly I say to you, I will drink no more of the fruit of the vine, until that day that I drink it new in the kingdom of God. When they had sung an hymn, they went out onto Mount Olives. Jesus says to them, All of you shall be offended because of Me this night: for it is written, I will strike the Shepherd, and the sheep shall be scattered. But after I am risen, I will go before you to Galilee. Peter says to Him, Although all shall be offended, yet will I not. Jesus says to him, Truly I say to you, This day, even on this night, before the rooster crow twice, you shall deny Me thrice. But he spoke the more vehemently, If I should die with You, I will not deny You in any case. Likewise also said they all. They came to a place which was named Gethsemane: and He says to His disciples, Sit here, while I pray. He takes with him Peter, James and John, and began to be sore amazed, and to be very heavy; and say to them, My soul is exceeding sorrowful unto death: linger here and watch. He went forward a little and fell on the ground, and prayed that, if it were possible, the hour might pass from Him. He says, Abba, Father, all things are possible for You; take away this cup from Me: nevertheless not My will, but Yours be done.

When Jesus finished all these sayings, He says to His disciples, you know that after two days is the feast of the passover, and the Son of Man is betrayed to be crucified. Then the chief priests, the scribes, and the elders of the people, assembled together at the palace of the high priest, who was called Caiaphas, to consult how they might take Jesus by subtlety, and kill Him. But they said, Not on the feast day, lest there be an uproar among the people. Now when Jesus was in Bethany, in the house of Simon the leper, There comes a woman having an alabaster box of very precious ointment, and pours it on His head, as He sits at meat. But when His disciples saw it, with indignation, they say, To what purpose is this waste? For this ointment might have been sold for much, and given to the poor. When Jesus understood it, He says to them, Why trouble you the woman? For she has done a good work on Me. For you have the poor always with you; but Me you have not always. She has poured this ointment on My body, for my burial. Truly I say to you, wherever this gospel is preached in the whole world, what this woman has done shall be told for a memorial of her. Then one of the twelve, called Judas Iscariot, goes to the chief priests, and say to them, What will you give me, and I will deliver Him to you? And they covenanted with him for thirty pieces of silver. From that time he sought an opportunity to betray Him. On the first day of the feast of unleavened bread the disciples come to Jesus, saying to Him, Where do You want us to prepare for You to eat the passover? And He says, Go into the city to such a man, and say to Him, The Master says, My time is at hand; I will keep the passover at your house with My disciples. And the disciples did as Jesus had appointed them; and they made ready the passover. Now when evening comes, He sits down with the twelve. As they eat, He says, Truly I say to you, that one of you shall betray Me. And they were exceeding sorrowful, and begin every one of them to say to Him, Master, is it I? And He answers and say, He who dips his hand with Me in the dish, the same shall betray Me. The Son of Man goes as it is written of Him: but woe unto that man by whom the Son of Man is betrayed! It would be good for that man if he had not been born. Then Judas, who betrays Him, answers and say, Master, is it I? He says to him, You have said it. And as they are eating, Jesus takes bread, blesses it and breaks it, and give it to the disciples, and say, Take, eat; this is My body. And He takes the cup, and gives thanks, and give it to them, saying, Drink all of it; For this is My blood of the new covenant, which is shed for many for the forgiveness of sins. But I say to you, I will not drink henceforth of this fruit of the vine, until that day when I drink it new with you in My Father's kingdom. When they had sung an hymn, they went out onto Mount Olives. Then Jesus says to them, All shall be offended because of Me this night: for it is written, I will strike the Shepherd, and the sheep of the flock shall scatter abroad. But after I am risen again, I will go before you into Galilee. Peter answers and say to Him, Though all men shall be offended because of You, yet I will never be offended. Jesus says to him, Truly I say to you, this night, before the rooster crow, you will deny Me thrice. Peter says to Him, Though I should die with You, yet will I not deny You. Likewise also said all the disciples. Then comes Jesus with them to a place called Gethsemane, and says to the disciples, Sit here, while I go and pray over there. He takes with Him Peter and the two sons of Zebedee, and begin to be sorrowful and very heavy. Then He says to them, My soul is exceeding sorrowful, even to death: linger here, and watch with Me. He goes a little further, and falls on His face, and prays, saying, O My Father, if it be possible, let this cup pass from Me: nevertheless not as I will, but Your will be done.

The woman who poured an expensive alabaster of ointment on Jesus' head was criticised for waste but commended by Jesus for anointing His body in advance for burial. It was a prophetic act of faith that Jesus would soon be rejected, betrayed and crucified as He taught. She took to heart Jesus' teaching of His passion, which the disciples somehow failed to understand and courageously acted without consulting anyone, risking being misunderstood.

What she has done will be spoken of whenever the gospel is preached throughout the world as a memorial of her singular act of lavish love in deepest gratitude for her Master's earthly ministry and gospel mission culminating in His momentous act of sacrifice on the cross. A glorious goodly death crowned by a fitting act of adorning His Head with one of earth's finest, fragrant and precious spikenard as His body lay in final repose and beautiful rest at last. If the seed did not die and is not buried, it will not yield fruit. If He did not die and was not buried, there is no resurrection from the dead. The Master who gave His life receives a perfect gift in return.

The Son of Man is Betrayed (14:37-72)

He comes and finding them sleeping, says to Peter, Simon, are you sleeping? Could you not watch one hour? Watch and pray, lest you enter into temptation. The spirit truly is ready, but the flesh is weak. Again He went away and prayed and spoke the same words. When He returned, He found them asleep again, (for their eyes were heavy,) nor know they how to answer Him. He comes the third time, and says to them, Sleep on now, and take your rest: it is enough, the hour is come; behold, the Son of Man is betrayed into the hands of sinners. Rise up, let us go; lo, he who betrays Me is at hand. Immediately, while He spoke, Judas, one of the twelve, come with a great multitude with swords and staves, from the chief priests, the scribes and the elders. He who betrayed Him had given them a token, saying, Whomever I kiss, that same is He; take Him, and lead Him away safely. As soon as he was come, he goes straightaway to Him, and say, Master, Master; and kissed Him. They laid their hands on Him, and took Him. One of them who stood by drew a sword, and smote a servant of the high priest, and cut off his ear. Jesus answers and say to them, Are you come out, as against a thief, with swords and with staves to take Me? I was daily with you in the temple teaching, and you took Me not: but the scriptures must be fulfilled. They all forsook Him, and fled. There followed Him a certain young man, having a linen cloth cast about his naked body; and the young men laid hold on him: He left the linen cloth, and fled from them naked. They led Jesus away to the high priest: and with him were assembled all the chief priests, elders and scribes. Peter followed Him afar off, even to the palace of the high priest: and he sat with the servants, and warmed himself at the fire. The chief priests and all the council sought for witness against Jesus to put Him to death; and found none. Many bore false witness against Him, but their witness agreed not together. There arose certain men, and bore false witness against Him, saying, We heard Him say, I will destroy this temple made with hands, and within three days I will build another made without hands. But neither did their witness agree together. The high priest stood up in the midst, and ask Jesus, saying, Answer You nothing? What is it which these witness against You? He held His peace, and answered nothing. Again the high priest ask Him, and says to Him, Are You the Messiah, the Son of the Blessed? Jesus says, I am: and you shall see the Son of Man sitting on the right hand of power, and coming in the clouds of heaven. The high priest rent his clothes, and say, What need we any further witnesses? You have heard the blasphemy: what think you? They all condemned Him to be guilty of death. Some spit on Him, cover His face and beat Him, saying to Him, Prophesy: and the servants strike Him with the palms of their hands. As Peter was beneath in the palace, there comes one of the maids of the high priest: when she saw Peter warming himself, she looked on him, and says, You also was with Jesus of Nazareth. But he denied, saying, I know not, neither understand what you say. And he went out into the porch; and the rooster crow. A maid sees him again, and begin to say to them who stood by, This is one of them. He denied it again. And a little after, those who stood by say again to Peter, Surely you are one of them: for you are a Galilaean, and your speech betrays you. But he begin to curse and to swear, saying, I know not this man of whom you speak. And the second time the rooster crow. Peter called to mind the word that Jesus said to Him, Before the rooster crow twice, you shall deny Me thrice. And when he thought about it more, he wept.

He comes to the disciples, and finds them asleep, and say to Peter, What, could you not watch with Me one hour? Watch and pray, that you enter not into temptation: the spirit indeed is willing, but the flesh is weak. He goes away again the second time, and pray, saying, O My Father, if this cup may not pass away from Me, except I drink it, Your will be done. And He comes and finds them asleep again: for their eyes are heavy. And He leaves them, and goes away again, and pray the third time, saying the same words. Then He comes to His disciples, and say to them, Sleep on now, and take your rest: behold, the hour is at hand, and the Son of Man is betrayed into the hands of sinners. Rise, let us be going: behold, he is at hand that betrays Me. And while He yet speaks, lo, Judas, one of the twelve, come, and with him a great multitude with swords and staves, from the chief priests and elders of the people. Now he that betrays Him give them a sign, saying, Whoever I shall kiss, that same is He: hold Him fast. And forthwith he comes to Jesus, and says, Hail, Master; and kisses Him. And Jesus says to him, Friend, why are you here? Then they come and lay hands on Jesus, and take Him. And, behold, one of them with Jesus stretch out his hand, and draws his sword, and strike a servant of the high priest's, and cut off his ear. Then Jesus says to Him, Put back again your sword into its place: for all they who takes the sword shall perish with the sword. Do you think I cannot now pray to My Father, and He shall presently give Me more than twelve legions of angels? But how then shall scriptures be fulfilled, that thus it must be? In that same hour Jesus says to the multitude, Are you come out as against a thief with swords and staves to take Me? I sat daily with you teaching in the temple, and you lay not hold on Me. But all this was done, that the scriptures of the prophets might be fulfilled. Then all the disciples forsake Him, and flee. And they who lay hold on Jesus lead Him away to Caiaphas the high priest, where the scribes and the elders assemble. But Peter follows Him afar off to the high priest's palace, and goes in, and sits with the servants, to see the end. Now the chief priests, elders, and all the council, seek false witnesses against Jesus, to put Him to death; but finds none: yes, though many false witnesses came forward, yet found none. At the last comes two false witnesses, and say, This fellow says, I am able to destroy the temple of God, and to build it in three days. And the high priest arise, and says to Him, Do You have nothing to say? What is it which these witness against You? But Jesus held His peace. And the high priest answers and say to Him, I adjure You by the living God, that You tell us whether You are the Messiah, the Son of God. Jesus says to him, You have said: nevertheless I say to you, Hereafter, you shall see the Son of Man sitting on the right hand of power, and coming in the clouds of heaven. Then the high priest rend his clothes, saying, He speaks blasphemy; what further need have we of witnesses? Behold, now you hear His blasphemy. What think you?

They answer and say, He is guilty of death. Then did they spit in His face, and buffet Him; and others strike Him with the palms of their hands, saying, Prophesy to us, You Messiah, who is he who strikes You? Now Peter sat outside in the palace ground: and a damsel comes to him, saying, You also are with Jesus of Galilee. But he denies before them all, saying, I know not what you say. And when he goes out into the porch, another maid sees him, and says to them who are there, This fellow is also with Jesus of Nazareth. And again he denies with an oath, I do not know the man. And after a while comes to him those standing by, and says to Peter, Surely you also are one of them; for your speech betrays you. He begin to curse and to swear, saying, I know not the man. Immediately the rooster crows. And Peter remembers the word of Jesus, which says to him, Before the rooster crow, you shall deny Me thrice. And he goes out, weeping bitterly. He was completely broken.

And the high priest answers and say to Him, I adjure You by the living God, that You tell us whether You are the Messiah, the Son of God? Jesus says to him, You have said: nevertheless I say to you, Hereafter, you shall see the Son of Man sitting on the right hand of power, and coming in the clouds of heaven. (Mt. 26:63-64)

For saying He is the Messiah, the Son of the living God and that they will see the Son of Man sitting at the right hand of power and coming in the clouds of heaven, before the high priest and a crowd of witnesses; Jesus is condemned for blasphemy worthy of death. In this, the council erred. The TaNaKh tell us that descendants of kings of Israel (Hebrew: prince of God) are princes, sons of David, hence, sons of God, pointing to His royal heritage and humanity.

Messiah Jesus, the Son of God, in His flesh is the Lamb of God as a momentous sacrifice; is also the Son of Man who now sits at the right hand of power. He is coming again in the clouds of heaven to judge the world at the end of the age. Will you reject, forsake and deny Him? Or, deny yourself, take up your cross and follow Him?

The King of the Jews (15:1-41)

Straightaway in the morning the chief priests consulted with the elders, scribes and the whole council; bound Jesus, carried and delivered Him to Pilate. Pilate ask Him, Are You the King of the Jews? He says to him, You say it. The chief priests accused Him of many things: but He answered nothing. Pilate ask Him again, saying, Answer You nothing? Behold how many things they witness against You. Jesus yet answered nothing; so that Pilate marvelled. Now at that feast he released to them one prisoner, whomever they desired. There was one named Barabbas, who lay bound with them that had made insurrection with him, and had committed murder in the insurrection. The multitude crying aloud began to desire him to do as he had ever done to them. But Pilate answers them, saying, Will you that I release to you the King of the Jews? He knew the chief priests had delivered Him out of envy. But the chief priests moved the people, that he should rather release Barabbas to them. Pilate answers and say again to them, What will you then that I do to Him whom you call the King of the Jews? They cry out again, Crucify Him. Pilate says to them, Why, what evil has He done? They cry out the more exceedingly, Crucify Him. And so Pilate, willing to make the people happy, released Barabbas to them and delivered Jesus, when he had scourged Him, to be crucified. The soldiers led him away into the hall, called Praetorium; and they call together the whole squad. They clothed Him with a purple robe, and put a crown of thorns on His head, and began to salute Him, Hail, King of the Jews! They struck Him on the head with a reed, spit on Him, and bowing their knees, worshipped Him. When they had mocked Him, they took off the purple robe from Him, and put His own clothes on Him, and led Him out to be crucified. They compel one Simon a Cyrenian, who passed by, coming out of the country, the father of Alexander and Rufus, to bear His cross. They bring Him to the place Golgotha, which is, being interpreted, The place of a skull. They gave Him to drink wine mingled with myrrh: but He received it not. When they had crucified Him, they parted His garments, casting lots upon them, what every man should take. It was 9AM when they crucified Him. And the superscription of His accusation was written over, THE KING OF THE JEWS. And with Him they crucify two thieves; one on His right hand, and the other on His left.

And the scripture was fulfilled, which says, And He was numbered with the transgressors. They that passed by railed on Him, wagging their heads, and saying, Ah, You who destroy the temple and build it in three days, deliver Yourself, and come down from the cross. Likewise also the chief priests mocking said among themselves with the scribes, He delivered others; Himself He cannot deliver. Let Messiah the King of Israel descend now from the cross, that we may see and believe. They who were crucified with Him reviled Him. When noon was come, there was darkness over the whole land until three o'clock. At that hour, Jesus cries with a loud voice, saying, Eloi, Eloi, lama sabachthani? which is, being interpreted, My God, My God, why have You forsaken Me? Some of them that stood by, when they heard it, says, Behold, he calls Elias. And one ran and filled a sponge full of vinegar, and put it on a reed, and gave Him to drink, saying, Let alone; let us see whether Elias will come to take Him down. Jesus cried with a loud voice, and gave up the ghost. And the veil of the temple was rent in two from the top to the bottom. And when the centurion, which stood over against Him, saw that He so cried out, and gave up the ghost, he said, Truly this man was the Son of God. There were also women looking on afar off: among whom was Mary Magdalene, and Mary the mother of James the younger and of Joses, and Salome; (Who also, when He was in Galilee, followed Him, and ministered to Him;) and many other women which came up with Him to Jerusalem.

When the morning comes. All the chief priests and elders of the people took counsel against Jesus to put Him to death. They bound Him, lead Him away and deliver Him to Pontius Pilate the governor.

Judas, who betrayed Him, saw that He was condemned, repented himself. He brought the thirty pieces of silver to the chief priests and elders, saying, I have sinned and betrayed innocent blood. They say, What is that to us? He cast down the pieces of silver in the temple, and goes and hang himself. The chief priests take the silver pieces, and say, It is not lawful to put them into the treasury, because this is blood money. They took counsel and bought the potter's field, to bury strangers in. Therefore the field is called, The field of blood till this day, fulfilling what was spoken by the prophet Jeremiah, And they took the thirty pieces of silver, the price of Him whom the children of Israel did value; the worth of a slave, and gave for the potter's field, as the Lord appointed Me.

Jesus stood before the governor. Are You the King of the Jews? Jesus says to him, You say. Do You not hear how many things they witness against You? He answers him not a word that the governor marvel greatly. When he set down on the judgment seat, his wife sends to him, saying, Have nothing to do with that righteous Man: for I suffered many things this day in a dream because of Him.

But the chief priests and elders persuade the multitude to ask for Barabbas and destroy Jesus. The governor answers and say to them, Which of the two will you that I release to you? They say, Barabbas. What shall I do with Jesus who is called Messiah? They all say to him, Crucify Him. Why, what evil has He done? They cry out even more, saying, Crucify Him. Pilate takes water and washes his hands before the multitude, saying, I am innocent of the blood of this righteous Person. Then answers all the people and say, His blood be on us and on our children. He releases Barabbas and when he has scourge Jesus, he delivers Him to be crucified.

The soldiers took Jesus into the common hall, gathering the squad of soldiers. They strip Him, put on Him a scarlet robe, made a crown of thorns, puts it on His head and a reed in His right hand. They bow the knee before Him and mock Him, saying, Hail, King of the Jews! They spit on Him, takes the reed and smites Him on the head. After they mock Him, they take the robe off Him, puts His own clothes on and lead Him away to crucify Him.

They found a man of Cyrene, Simon: compels him to bear His cross. They come to a place called Golgotha, that is, a place of a skull, gives Him vinegar mingled with gall: but after tasting it, He refuses it. They crucify Him, divided His garments, casting lots:

fulfilling what was spoken by the prophet: They divided My garments among them, and on My vesture did they cast lots.

Sitting down, they watched Him there; set up over His head His accusation writes, THIS IS JESUS THE KING OF THE JEWS. Two thieves they crucify with Him, one on His right hand, the other on His left. Those who passes by revile Him, wagging their heads, You who destroy the temple, and build it in three days, deliver Yourself. If You are the Son of God, come down from the cross.

Likewise the chief priests mocking Him, with the scribes and elders, say, He delivers others; Himself He cannot deliver. If He is the King of Israel, let Him now come down from the cross, and we will believe Him. He trusts in God; let Him deliver Him now, if He will have Him: for He says, I am the Son of God.

Darkness covers all the land from noon till three o'clock. About that time, Jesus cries with a loud voice, saying, Eli, Eli, lama sabachthani? that is to say, My God, my God, why have You forsaken Me? Some standing there says, This man calls for Elias. Let us see if Elias will come to save Him. Jesus, when He cries again with a loud voice, yields up the spirit.

My God, My God, why have You forsaken Me? All who see Me laugh Me to scorn: they shake the head, saying, He trusted on the Lord that He would deliver Him: let Him deliver Him, seeing He delighted in Him. They pierced My hands and My feet. They part My garments among them, and cast lots upon My vesture. (Psalm 22)

And, behold, the veil of the temple was torn in two from the top to the bottom; the earth quake, the rocks break. And graves open; many bodies of the saints who sleep rise and come out of the graves after His resurrection, and goes into the holy city, and appear to many. When the centurion and those with him watching Jesus, saw the earthquake and those things that are done, they fear greatly, saying, Truly this is the Son of God.

He Is Risen (15:42-16:20)

When the evening comes, because it was the preparation, that is, the day before the sabbath, Joseph of Arimathaea, an honourable counsellor, who also waited for the kingdom of God, came, and went in boldly to Pilate, and asked for the body of Jesus. Pilate wondered if He were really dead: and calling to him the centurion, he asked him whether He had been dead for awhile. When he knew it of the centurion, he gave the body to Joseph, who bought fine linen, and took Him down, wrapped Him in the linen, and laid Him in a sepulchre which was hewn out of a rock, and rolled a stone unto the door of the sepulchre. And Mary Magdalene and Mary the mother of Joses beheld where He was laid.

When the sabbath was past, Mary Magdalene, and Mary the mother of James, and Salome, bought sweet spices, to come and anoint Him. Very early in the morning on the first day of the week, they came to the sepulchre at the rising of the sun. They said among themselves, Who shall roll away the stone from the door of the sepulchre? When they looked, they saw that the stone was rolled away: for it was very great. Entering into the sepulchre, they saw a young man sitting on the right side, clothed in a long white garment; and they were terrified. He says to them, Be not afraid: You seek Jesus of Nazareth, who was crucified: He is risen; He is not here: behold the place where they laid Him. But go your way, tell His disciples and Peter that He goes before you into Galilee: there you shall see Him, as He said to you. They went out quickly, and fled from the sepulchre; for they trembled and were amazed: neither said they anything to any one; for they were afraid.

When Jesus was risen early the first day of the week, He appeared first to Mary Magdalene, whom He had cast out seven devils. She went and told those who had been with Him, as they mourned and wept. When they heard He was alive and had been seen by her, believed not. After that He appeared in another form to two of them, as they went into the countryside. They went and told the rest: neither believed they them. Afterward He appeared to the eleven as they sat at meat, and rebuked them for their unbelief and hardness of heart, because they believed not those who had seen Him after He was risen. He says to them, Go into all the world, and preach the gospel to every creature. He who believes and is baptised shall be delivered; but he who believes not shall be damned. These signs shall follow those who believe; In My Name they shall cast out devils; speak with new tongues; take up serpents; any deadly thing they drink shall not hurt them; they shall lay hands on the sick, and they shall recover. After the Master had spoken to them, He was received up into heaven, and sat on the right hand of God. They went forth, and preached everywhere, the Master working with them, and confirming the word with signs following. Amen.

When the evening comes, Joseph of Arimathaea, a rich man, who himself is Jesus' disciple, goes to Pilate, and begs the body of Jesus. Pilate commands the body to be delivered. When Joseph has taken the body, he wraps it in a clean linen cloth, and lays it in his own new tomb, which he hews out in the rock: and he rolls a great stone to the door of the sepulchre. Mary Magdalene and the other Mary, sits over against the sepulchre.

The next day, follows the day of preparation, the chief priests and Pharisees come together to Pilate, saying, Sir, we remember that deceiver says, while He was yet alive, After three days I will rise again. Command therefore the sepulchre be made sure until the third day, lest His disciples come by night, and steal Him away, and say to the people, He is risen from the dead: so the last error shall be worse than the first. Pilate says to them, You have a watch: go your way, make it as sure as you can. So they went, and made the sepulchre sure, sealing the stone, and setting a watch.

At the end of the sabbath, as it begins to dawn toward the first day of the week, Mary Magdalene and the other Mary comes to see the sepulchre. Behold, there is a great earthquake: for the angel of the Lord descends from heaven, and come and roll back the stone from the door, and sits upon it. His countenance is like lightning, and his clothes white as snow: And for fear of him the keepers did shake, and become as dead men.

The angel answers and say to the women, Fear not: for I know you seek Jesus, who was crucified. He is not here: He is risen, as He says. Come, see the place where the Lord lay. Go quickly, tell His disciples He is risen from the dead.

Behold, He goes before you into Galilee; there you shall see Him: lo, I have told you. They departed quickly from the sepulchre with fear and great joy; running to bring His disciples word. As they went to tell His disciples, behold, Jesus meets them, saying, All hail. And they come and hold Him by the feet, and worship Him. Then says Jesus to them, Be not afraid: go tell My brothers that they go into Galilee, and there they shall see Me. When they went, behold, some of the watch comes into the city, and shows the chief priests all the things that are done. When they assembled with the elders, and taken counsel, they gave a large sum of money to the soldiers, saying, Say you, His disciples came by night, and stole Him away while we slept. And if this comes to the governor's ears, we will persuade him, and secure you. So they took the money, and did as they are taught: and this saying is commonly reported among the Jews until this day. Then the eleven disciples went away into Galilee, into a mountain where Jesus appointed them. When they saw Him, they worshipped Him but some doubted.

That same day, Jesus appeared to two men on the road to Emmaus who did not recognise Him at first, until He spoke with them. He says to them, O fools, and slow of heart to believe all that the prophets have spoken: Ought not Messiah to have suffered these things, and enter into His glory? Beginning at Moses and all the prophets, He expounded to them in all the scriptures the things concerning Himself. And it came to pass, as He sat at the table with them, He took bread and blessed it, broke and gave to them. And their eyes opened, and they knew Him; and He vanished out of their sight. And they say one to another, Did not our heart burn within us, while He talks with us by the way, and while He opened to us the scriptures?

And they rose up the same hour, and returned to Jerusalem, and found the eleven gathered together, and those with them, saying, The Master is risen indeed, and has appeared to Simon. As they tell what things are done in the way, and how He was known by them in breaking of bread, Jesus Himself stood in the midst of them, and says to them, Peace be to you. But they were terrified and trembled, and supposed they were seeing a spirit. And He says to them, Why are you troubled? And why do thoughts arise in your hearts? Behold My hands and My feet, that it is I Myself: touch Me, and see; for a spirit has not flesh and bones, as you see Me have. And when He thus speaks, He showed them His hands and His feet. And while they yet believe not for joy, and wonder, He says to them, Have you here any meat? They gave Him a piece of a broiled fish, and an honeycomb. He takes it, and eat before them. He says to them, These are the words which I spoke to you, while I was yet with you, that all things must be fulfilled, which are written in the law of Moses, and in the prophets, and in the psalms, concerning Me. Then He opened their mind, that they might understand the scriptures, and says to them, Thus it is written, and therefore it was necessary for Messiah to suffer, and to rise from the dead the third day: and that repentance and forgiveness of sins shall be preached in His Name among all nations, beginning at Jerusalem. And you are witnesses of these things. Behold, I send the promise of My Father upon you: but linger in the city of Jerusalem, until you are endued with power from on high.

All authority is given to Me in heaven and on earth. Go therefore, and teach all nations, baptising them in the Name of the Father, and of the Son, and of the Holy Spirit: Teaching them to observe all things whatever I have commanded you: and, lo, I am with you always, even unto the end of the age. Amen.

I saw in the night visions,
ONE LIKE THE SON OF MAN
on the clouds of heaven,
come to the Ancient of days,
they brought him near to him.
He was given dominion,
and glory, and a kingdom,
all people, nations, languages,
shall serve him: his dominion
is an everlasting dominion,
which shall not pass away,
his kingdom shall not be ruin.
—Daniel 7:13-14

Epilogue

While Psalm 8 praises the Son of Man as the apex of God's creation, God calls Ezekiel by this enigmatic term (more than 90 times) to both condemn Israel's sins and captivity but also deliverance and new life through the Spirit by an everlasting covenant of peace establishing the reign of the Son of David, the Servant King forever. Consequently, Daniel foresaw in a vision the Son of Man as an exalted heavenly figure given a kingdom, power and glory, where all people, nations, and languages serve Him, whose dominion is everlasting and whose kingdom is unshakable.

It was no wonder that some Jews tried to forcibly make Jesus king as a political ruler to deliver them from Roman subjection and drove Judas to betray Him and later to suicide when it became apparent that Jesus meant to have rule in the hearts of souls, and not an earthly dominion as King of the Jews, Messiah king of Israel.

Furthermore, Jesus did not come to establish a new religious order but to renew the covenant relationship between the God of Abraham, Isaac and Jacob and His people as the promised Messiah, Son of the living God, spoken by Israel's prophets to deliver them from futility of striving for Mosaic righteousness to resting in Messianic righteousness by faith in the risen Master Jesus who delivered us from death by His great sacrifice as the Lamb of God taking away the sins of the world and proclaimed in the gospel of the kingdom of God. For though the law is good and holy, it cannot make us good and holy but the word of grace and faith in Messiah Jesus through the Holy Spirit made us righteous to newness of life.

As disciple practitioners and children of God, the path to greatness is servanthood, not tyranny and true leadership is to be a slave of all, not lording over, for even the Son of Man did not come to be served, but to serve, and to give His life a ransom for many.

He is no fool
who gives what he cannot keep
to gain what he cannot lose.

What More Could A Man Ask

I walked out to the hill just now.

It is exalting, delicious, to stand embraced by the shadows of a friendly tree with the wind tugging at your coattail and the heavens hailing your heart, to gaze and glory and give oneself again to God—what more could a man ask?

Oh, the fullness, pleasure, sheer excitement of knowing God on earth! I care not if I never raise my voice again for him, if only I may love him, please him.

Perhaps in mercy he shall give me a host of children that I may lead them through the vast star fields to explore his delicacies whose finger ends set them to burning.

But if not, if only I may see him, touch his garments, and smile into his eyes—ah then, not stars nor children shall matter, only himself.

O Jesus, Master and Centre and End of all, how long before that glory is yours which has so long awaited you?

Now there is no thought of you among men; then there shall be thought for nothing else.

Now other men are praised; then none shall care for any other's merits.

Hasten, hasten, Glory of Heaven, take your crown, subdue your kingdom, enthral your creatures.

> He is no fool who gives what he cannot keep
> to gain what he cannot lose.

Jim Elliot

How to Read this Book

1. "Everything we see hides another thing, we always want to see what is hidden by what we see." What did Magritte mean? Are there other interpretations & meanings?

2. Is Christianity a departure or continuity of Judaism?

3. What did the author mean by: "God delight not only in good work but desire to make us holy and good as He is" in the passage on Good News of Good Life?

4. Do you agree that greatness is characterise by servanthood and true leadership is define as being a slave of all?

5. Consider each of the 30 readings in light of what it means to understand the different titles used by Mark of Jesus: Jesus of Nazareth, Holy One of God, Son of Man, Lord of Sabbath, Son of God, Son of the Most High God. Also, Carpenter, Son of Mary, Prophet, Beloved Son, Good Master, Messiah Son of David, Messiah Son of the Blessed, King of the Jews, Messiah King of Israel. Who do others say Jesus is? Who do you say He is?

6. Why did the people conclude that Jesus taught with authority and receive His teaching gladly as compared to the scribes and the other religious authorities?

7. What is meant by "New Wine Must Be Put Into New Wineskin"? Why did Jesus gave new surnames to some of His disciples?

8. What is the leaven of the Pharisees and the leaven of Herod Jesus warn His disciples to beware? (Mk. 8:15) Do you agree with the author's explanation? Are there other possible views?

9. What does it mean for Jesus to have the power not only to do mighty works, but also the authority to forgive sins, command the sea to be still and the wind to cease and they obey Him?

10. What is the gospel of Messiah Jesus and the kingdom of God? Are the 5 characteristics Jesus pointed concerning the Son of Man: rejection, betrayal, death, burial, and resurrection also to be found in outliers and followers of our Master Messiah Jesus?

Readers may write to me here: outlier@outlook.sg

Made in the USA
Monee, IL
21 December 2020